EAT & EXPLORE

Illinois

Cookbook & Travel Guide

EAT & EXPLORE *Illinois*

Cookbook & Travel Guide

by Anita Musgrove

Great American Publishers

www.GreatAmericanPublishers.com

TOLL-FREE 1-888-854-5954

Great American Publishers

501 Avalon Way Suite B • Brandon, MS 39047

TOLL-FREE 1-888-854-5954 • www.GreatAmericanPublishers.com

ISBN 978-1-934817-32-2

FIRST EDITION

10 9 8 7 6 5 4 3 2 1

by Anita Musgrove

Cover: Map © The National Atlas of the United States of America • Compass © scanrail • Skyline © pawel.gaul • Chicago dog © LauriPatterson • Bridge © Dennis Slape • Illinois state shape © korhankaracan • Inside pages: Inside background © dziewul • Illinois waterfall © EJ_Rodriquez • Chicago skyline © marchello74 • Bruschetta © sumnersgraphicsinc • Pretzels © LauriPatterson • French Toast © James Stefuik • Zucchini Pie © peredniankina • Soup © Funwithfood • Vegetable basket © Jasmina007 • Meat © Magone • Dessert © edoneil

Contents

Introduction

Eat & Explore Illinois—the eighth edition to the EAT & EXPLORE STATE COOKBOOK SERIES—has been a labor of love. Each book in the series is a year-long process of getting to know the state and her people. So far, we have completed Arkansas, Minnesota, North Carolina, Ohio, Oklahoma, Virginia and Washington, and it's always an adventure discovering the next state. My work is so much fun that if I didn't make a living at it, I would never believe it's a job.

Our goal with the Eat & Explore books is that you experience each state like never before.... That you get to know the heart of the state—just as we do—as you explore the flavors that make the state special and discover the state's communities, celebrations, and destinations that are waiting for your enjoyment

Illinois, nicknamed "the Prairie State," has so much to offer. It's marked by farmland, forests, rolling hills and wetlands. Chicago, one of the largest cities in the United States sits on the shore of Lake Michigan and is famous for its skyscrapers like Willis Tower and Tribune Tower. While 3 presidents were elected while living in Illinois, Abraham Lincoln, Ulysses S. Grant and Barack Obama, only one president, Ronald Reagan, was actually born and raised in Illinois. He was elected while living in California.

There is much to love about Illinois, and the nearest and dearest things are those that take me back to my childhood. Like the fact you can find a brass statue of Popeye in Sugar Park (page 123) overlooking the Mississippi River. Chester, Illinois, home of Popeye creator, Elzie Crisler Sega, has an Annual Popeye Festival every September to honor the beloved Sailor Man.

Burl Ives was born in Jasper County, which is featured on page 135. Burl Ives has been one of my favorite stars for years. He was both a singer and a star in movies like *Summer Magic* with Haley Mills and is well-known as the voice of Sam the Snowman in *Rudolph the Red-Nosed Reindeer*. No one has a voice as famous as Burl Ives, in my opinion.

In Metropolis (page 97), where heroes and history meet on the shores of the Ohio River, you can tour the Superman Museum and visit the 15-foot bronze statue in the middle of Superman Square. While there, you may want to take a walk through the underwater Boeing 727 airplane.

Because one person does not a team make, I must recognize my awesome co-workers at Great American Publishers. Thank you Heather Bowman and Victoria Renegar for your dedication and for giving this book wings. Brooke Craig and Diane Rothery thank you for the leadership. Christina Jo Campbell, Christy Campbell, Tory Hackett, LeeAnn Leach, Tasha Monk, Zak Simmons, Nichole Stewart, and Daniel Wyndham you all work together to make this book possible; thank you. But most of all God is our driving focus; without Him nothing is possible and I am thankful for His hand in this book.

My special thanks goes to the special man in my life, Richard Shaw. Thank you for putting up with my bad attitude when the book's not going exactly as planned and thank you for sharing the good days when we are traveling states to meet, greet and sign books. (Take my word for it, he's awesome.) Thank you, from the bottom of my heart, to my daughter, Sheila and her husband Roger, the owners of Great American Publishers. You always have the faith and words of encouragement to help me through each day as I try to make each thing I touch and do in my life be a glory to God. Family means everything. Sheila and my son Mickey along with their families—Roger, Nic, Ryan, Shelbie and Trace, Frankie, Brooke, Bryce, and Morgan—are my blessings and highest praise I give to God.

I am thankful too for each of you who buys the book, cooks the recipes and visits the places featured. Buckle your seat belt and let's hit the road and start eating and exploring our way through Illinois. Man this is going to be a great trip!

Anita Musgrove

Beverages & Appetizers

Mango Kale Smoothie

1 banana
1 cup kale, fresh or frozen
1 cup frozen mango
2 cups water, milk or milk substitute
1 tablespoon lemon juice
1 tablespoon fresh ginger, optional

Put all ingredients in a blender. Blend to your desired consistency.

Anicca Float Club

Photos for Anicca Float Club courtesy of Groupon Photographers

Anicca Float Club

4S100 IL Route 59 • Suite 6 • Naperville, IL 60563
630-854-7385 • www.aniccafloatclub.com • Find us on Facebook

Have you ever wanted to try meditation but don't have the time or can't sit still? Are your muscles sore from that hard workout you did? Do you struggle with arthritis or chronic pain? Let your mind and body take a vacation for an hour. Float away from your worries and experience the equivalent of four hours of sleep in one hour of flotation. Flotation therapy is an experience like nothing else. When was the last time you floated weightlessly in a quiet place with nothing but the sound of your own breath? Float and relax in an 8x6-foot tub filled with ten inches of water and 1,600 pounds of pharmaceutical-grade Epsom salt making it impossible to sink. The solution is heated to the temperature of your skin, removing 90% of the sensation of gravity from your body. This combination is profoundly relaxing for the central nervous system, allowing the mind to slide into a deeply meditative state known as theta state. Flotation therapy depresses stress hormones, lowers blood pressure, promotes circulation, relieves pain, and reduces anxiety. Meet Anicca Float Club.

Monday: 4:00 pm to 9:00 pm
Tuesday–Saturday: 10:00 am to 8:00 pm
Sunday: 10:00 am to 5:00 pm

Fruit Punch

2 cups crushed pineapple
3 cups water
3 to 4 cups sugar
6 lemons, juiced
6 oranges, juiced
1 cup maraschino cherry juice
1 cup chopped maraschino cherries
2 quarts cold tea
2 quarts ginger ale
1 pint grape juice

In a saucepan, boil pineapple, water and sugar 15 minutes; cool. Add lemon, orange and cherry juices along with cherries and tea. Just before serving, add ginger ale and grape juice. Pour over ice in a punch bowl. Makes 40 servings.

Something Sweet

Something Sweet ships anywhere in the United States!

891 Main Street • Antioch, IL 60002
847-838-9350 • www.4somethingsweet.com • Find us on Facebook

Something Sweet specializes in delivering a homemade taste right to you from Main Street in downtown Antioch. Stacked floor to ceiling, this candy shop offers a variety of confections and is famous for their fudge, Bearfoots, chocolate bark, and truffles. This storefront confectionary also features a vast selection of old-fashioned penny candies for the nostalgic at heart, as well as gourmet chocolates, taffy apples, and ice cream. Something Sweet is the perfect place to buy gifts for wedding showers and special event favors, as well as corporate gifting. Voted "Best Candy Shop" in Chicago in 2013, their selections and customer service make this stop worth making. Orders can be placed in person or by phone, so if you are looking for Something Sweet, you've found it!

Sunday, Tuesday & Wednesday: Noon to 5:00 pm
Thursday & Friday: Noon to 8:00 pm
Saturday: 10:00 am to 8:00 pm

Punch

1 (.13-ounce) pack cherry Kool-Aid
1 (.13-ounce) pack strawberry Kool-Aid
2 cups sugar
12 cups water
1 (6-ounce) can frozen orange juice, defrosted
1 (6-ounce) can frozen lemonade, defrosted
1 quart ginger ale

In a large container, mix Kool-Aids, sugar, water and juices; stir to mix well. Just before serving, add ginger ale. Makes 1½ gallons.

Long Hollow Canopy Tours

Pine Needle Tea

24 white pine needles
2 cups water

Make a bundle of needles (new green needles in summer work best); cut off brown ends. In a saucepan, bring water to a boil; add needles. Reduce heat; simmer 15 minutes. Remove needles and serve immediately for hot tea or cool and pour over ice for iced tea. Experiment with amounts of water and needles to suit individual taste.

Black Hawk State Historic Site

Frozen Hot Chocolate with Italian Meringue

You will need a candy or digital probe thermometer to make the Italian Meringue, but it is worth the small effort. The result is a delicious, creamy, fluffy "marshmallow" topping you can toast with a food torch. Alternatively, you can top the chocolate with chocolate curls, whipped cream or a dollop of store-bought marshmallow cream.

Chocolate:

12 ounces good quality dark chocolate, chopped
2 teaspoons cocoa
2 tablespoons sugar (3 tablespoons for a sweeter taste)
1½ cups whole milk, divided
3 cups ice

Melt chocolate in a large bowl over a double boiler. Add cocoa and sugar, stirring to combine completely. Remove from heat and slowly add ½ cup milk. Stir until smooth. Cool to room temperature or refrigerate until ready to use. (While mix is cooling, you can start Italian Meringue.) Once chocolate mix is cool, put in a blender, and add remaining milk and ice. Blend on high to desired consistency.

Italian Meringue:

¾ cup sugar
¼ cup water
1½ tablespoons light corn syrup, divided
3 large egg whites, room temperature

Combine sugar, water and 1 tablespoon corn syrup in a small saucepan; cook sugar syrup to 118°. While syrup is cooking, combine egg whites and remaining corn syrup in the bowl of a stand mixer; whip on high just until it is foamy and looks like shaving cream, but do not over whip. When desired consistency is reached, turn mixer down to low speed. When syrup reaches 118°, immediately stream liquid down side of bowl slowly without hitting whisk so that hot syrup does not splash out of bowl. When all syrup has been added, turn mixer to high speed; whip until mixture is white, fluffy, and the bowl is cool to touch. To serve, pour chocolate mix in serving glass. Top with Italian Meringue. Toast meringue with a brûlée torch. Serve frozen hot chocolate with a striped straw and spoon.

Whimsical Candy

Summer Sangria

This refreshing sangria is the perfect drink for a summer day or moonlit night. It is easy to make so you can spend time with family and friends. Relax and enjoy.

1 bottle Twelve Oaks Vineyard Chambourcin wine
1 (12-ounce) can frozen juice concentrate (choose your flavor, we like berry blend or
    blueberry pomegranate)
2 cans cold water (using can from juice concentrate)
2 cans ginger ale (using can from juice concentrate)
Fresh fruit for garnish (strawberries, blueberries, oranges, limes, etc.)

In a large pitcher, mix all ingredients together except fruit garnish. Garnish with fresh fruit. Cool in refrigerator so flavors meld. Serve over ice. This is also great to freeze and have ready for a quick party with family and friends.

Twelve Oaks Vineyard

Photos courtesy of www.traditionsportraitdesign.com

Twelve Oaks Vineyard

18975 Vogel Road • Carlyle, IL 62231

618-594-7459 • www.twelveoaksvineyard.com • Find us on Facebook

At Twelve Oaks Vineyard, they believe in offering quality wines that are handcrafted in the beautiful country outside the southern Illinois town of Carlyle. The grapes grown in this charming vineyard are maintained and cared for by a small family-owned business. The reserve wines humbly wear the label of the varieties of grapes grown in the vineyard. Their customers are encouraged to enjoy the fruit flavors in the wines and relax in a country setting with family and friends. Above all, Twelve Oaks Vineyard always gives thanks to God for the blessings that He gives in the little gifts of each day.

Saturday & Sunday: 1:00 pm to 6:00 pm
Monday–Friday: By Appointment

Commit to the Lord whatever you do,
and He will establish your plans.
—Proverbs 16:3

Bennet Mill Blizzard

1½ ounces Bennett Mill Bourbon™
1½ ounces cranberry juice
½ ounce lime juice
½ ounce grenadine
1 teaspoon sugar
Ice

Add all ingredients to a cocktail shaker. Shake until combined; pour into a cocktail glass with ice. Brrr!

Fox River Distilling Company

Fox River Distilling Company

204 Dearborn Court #110 • Geneva, IL 60134
630-402-0027 • www.foxriverdistilling.com

Fox River Distilling Company produces premium, handcrafted artisan spirits using traditional distilling methods. They consistently win awards for their outstanding Herrington Premium Vodka, Herrington Geneva's Gin, and Bennett Mill Bourbon from such notable events as the San Francisco World Spirits Competition, the Heartland Spirits Fest and Whiskey Competition, and many others. The actual working distillery is located near the Northern Illinois Food Bank in the Geneva Business Park. The distillery operates seven days a week, with tours offered on Friday and Saturday afternoons for a nominal fee. FRDC also hosts its legendary "First Friday," a monthly open house, where the distillery and tasting room are open to the public for extended hours, providing an up close and social opportunity to visit with friends or family. A mini tour is always part of the night, and local restaurants are invited on a rotating schedule to showcase their recipes and provide samples using Fox River Distilling Company spirits. Live music from local artists, and local merchants are invited to display their products at selected times during the year. Sign up at WWW.FOXRIVERDISTILLING. COM for monthly newsletter to get insider information about events, new product releases, and specials.

Friday: Noon to 6:00 pm; Tours at 4:00 pm & 5:00 pm
Saturday: Noon to 5:00 pm; Tours at 2:00 pm & 4:00 pm

KOVAL Vodka Cosmopolitan

Splash cranberry juice
2 ounces KOVAL vodka
1 ounce Cointreau
1 ounce fresh lime juice
Ice
1 orange twist, garnish

In a cocktail glass, add splash cranberry juice. In a shaker, combine vodka, Cointreau, lime juice and ice; shake 20 times. Strain over cranberry juice in cocktail glass. Garnish with orange twist.

KOVAL Distillery

KOVAL Distillery

5121 North Ravenswood Avenue • Chicago, IL 60640
312-878-7988 • 312-465-3788 daytime
www.koval-distillery.com

KOVAL is one of America's largest artisan distilleries and winner of over fifty international awards. KOVAL pioneered a new school of distilling in the United States that focuses on using only the heart cut of the distillate. The heart cut is the purest, most grain-forward portion of the distillate, affording KOVAL its signature clean, bright style. KOVAL is also known for its use of unique and interesting grains, inspiring Wine Enthusiast to name the distillery a "leader of the alt-grain scene." All of KOVAL's whiskies are single barrel and aged in thirty-gallon barrels of new American oak, and in turn, each bottle can be traced back to the field on which the grain was grown. All of KOVAL's whiskey, gin, vodka, and liqueurs are certified organic and kosher and made from grain to bottle in Chicago.

Tours
Wednesday: 7:00 pm
Saturday: 1:00 pm, 2:00 pm, 3:00 pm, 4:00 pm, 5:00 pm
Sunday: 2:00 pm, 3:00 pm, 4:00 pm

Retail Hours
Monday–Friday: 2:00 pm to 7:00 pm
Saturday: 1:00 pm to 6:30 pm
Sunday: 2:00 pm to 5:00 pm

Red Dragon Hot Wassail

1 orange
12 whole cloves
2 bottles Mackinaw Valley Vineyard Red Dragon Wine
1 quart cranberry juice
1 quart apple juice
2 cinnamon sticks

Pierce orange with cloves. Combine all ingredients in slow cooker to warm at least 1 hour before serving. Makes 14 (8-ounce) servings.

Mackinaw Valley Vineyard

Mackinaw Valley Vineyard

Open 2nd Weekend in February through December

33633 State Route 9 • Mackinaw, IL 61755
309-359-9463 • www.MackinawValleyVineyard.com
Facebook- MackinawWinery

The Hahn family looks forward to welcoming you to Mackinaw Valley Vineyard and Winery, a year-round destination conveniently located a short drive from Peoria, Bloomington-Normal, and surrounding communities. The eighty-six-acre property is a working vineyard and winery situated on a glacial moraine with a thirty-mile valley view from the tasting room and decks. Visitors often say they feel that they've been on a mini vacation when they visit the vineyard, taste the award-winning wines, and spend a relaxing day in the country. The Vineyard hosts Saturday summer concerts, three summer festivals, murder mystery dinners, painting classes, and trivia game nights as well as many parties, weddings, and receptions. Come and experience one of Illinois's most picturesque destinations, or as they like to say, "Wine country in our own backyard."

Vino Drizzle

1¼ cups red grapes
½ cup tree cranberries
1 tablespoon brown sugar
¼ cup water
½ cup Veronica's Vino Drizzle
1 (10-ounce) Brie wheel
Thymes leaves for garnish
2 tablespoons pine nuts, toasted
1 loaf French bread, warmed

Preheat oven to 350°. In a medium saucepan over medium heat, combine grapes, cranberries, sugar and water; bring to a simmer. Cool 15 minutes, stirring occasionally, until fruit is tender and syrup forms; stir in wine drizzle. Place Brie on parchment paper-lined baking sheet. Spread fruit compote over top. Bake 10 to 12 minutes so cheese begins to soften. Garnish with thyme leaves. Serve with pine nuts and French bread.

Fergedaboudit Vineyard and Winery

Fergedaboudit
Vineyard & Winery

4595 West Speer Road • Hanover, IL 61041
815-591-2126 • www.fergedaboudit.com

Looking for a nice, relaxing day as you travel through Illinois? Visit Fergedaboudit Vineyard and Winery in Hanover. Take in the view of the rolling hills of the countryside as you enjoy a sampling of several Italian-inspired wines with an antipasto or cheese plate, and listen to musical guests perform during the summer months. View the tasting room designed to evoke memories of a Tuscan wine village. Some of the current available wine varieties include Cabernet Franc, Syrah, Sangiovese, and Moscato in addition to specialty wine products, such as Frezzie De Vino, a frozen cocktail mix, and Veronica's Vino Drizzle, a sweet concentrated wine syrup meant to be enjoyed over cheese, fruit, and desserts. All of the wines can be purchased online and shipped to select states. The vineyard's lush romantic setting makes it perfect for weddings, and the grounds may be rented for special events and private parties.

Thursday, Friday & Sunday: 11:00 am to 4:30 pm
Saturday: 11:00 am to 6:00 pm

Jezebel Sauce

This little sauce is used for topping our Brie. It was very popular back in the 1970's in southern Louisiana. It was said that no self-respecting host would be caught dead without Jezebel in the refrigerator! It was quick and easy to use when impromptu guests would arrive. Hosts and hostesses would top a block of cream cheese and serve crackers with it. Here at the Rhythm Kitchen, our friends and neighbors enjoy it over our Brie. Try it for yourself!

1 (18-ounce) jar apple jelly
1 (18-ounce) jar pineapple preserves
¼ cup dry mustard
⅛ cup ground horseradish
½ tablespoon coarse black pepper
1 wheel Brie

Place all ingredients except Brie into a food processor; blend until smooth. Refrigerate overnight to let flavors marry. It'll keep for a week and a few days due to its high acidity. Serve over Brie. Enjoy!

Chef Jason Zeck
Rhythm Kitchen Music Café

Enjoy Peoria

456 Fulton Street • Peoria, IL 61602
309-676-0303 • www.enjoypeoria.com • Find us on Facebook

Enjoy Peoria is a Conventions and Visitors Bureau (CVB), a nonprofit destination marketing organization that provides information about a specific destination. From providing brochures, maps, and discounts to inviting convention attendees, delegations, and sporting events to our communities, CVBs are a great resource for local businesses and pleasure travelers. Enjoy Peoria's mission is to promote the Peoria area as a destination and contribute to the economic growth of the communities represented. Enjoy Peoria helps promote local partner businesses and services through a number of mediums, including its annual Peoria Area Experience Guide and newly redesigned website. Through its tourism department, convention sales, sports, and marketing, Enjoy Peoria is a one-stop shop for discovering everything the Peoria area has to offer.

Monday–Friday: 8:30 am to 5:00 pm

Image courtesy of Dennis Slape

Fried Wings

12 small chicken wings
¼ teaspoon seasoned salt
1 cup all-purpose flour
1 teaspoon coarse salt
½ teaspoon black pepper
¼ teaspoon cayenne pepper
¼ teaspoon paprika
1 cup buttermilk
2 quarts vegetable oil

Season chicken with seasoned salt. In a wide shallow bowl, mix all dry ingredients; set aside. In another wide shallow bowl, pour buttermilk. Press wings into flour mixture to coat, dip in buttermilk and into flour again. Place on a rack, without wings touching, to rest 15 to 30 minutes. For thicker crust dredge in flour again; rest another 15 minutes before frying. In a deep skillet or fryer, heat oil to 375°. Cook 9 to 12 minutes or until juices run clear. Drain wings on rack. Pack into your favorite resealable container and watch the looks on your family's faces when you open the dish to eat.

The WLWSST is proud of its history of professional water-skiers performing all across the world including ski shows at Sea World, Cypress Gardens, Tommy Bartlett's, Water Ski Show Inc. World Entertainment, and many others. Our skiers have performed for professional shows in Florida, Ohio, California, Louisiana, New Jersey, Wisconsin, Australia, Germany, Malaysia, Japan, and others.

Wonder Lake Water Ski Show Team

Memorial Day through Labor Day

Corner of Hancock Drive and East Lakeshore Drive • Wonder Lake, IL 60097
www.wonderlakeskiteam.org • Find us on Facebook

Most people wouldn't think of the Midwest as a powerhouse for waterskiing, but from a small town in northeastern Illinois comes a big water-ski show team. The Wonder Lake Water Ski Show Team are five-time National Champions, and have been thrilling crowds in Wonder Lake and the surrounding areas for more than fifty years. Human Pyramids, Barefooting, Freestyle Jumping, and Water Ballet are acts you can expect to see when taking in a show. The best part is that the shows are free! Grab a lawn chair or blanket, a cooler full of your favorite beverages, your sunglasses, and come enjoy the show. Shows are most Friday nights at 7:00 pm during the summer, from Memorial Day through Labor Day. Please check the website for the most up-to-date information and calendar of events. Shows take place on the east side of Wonder Lake, at Wonder Center Beach, located at the corner of Hancock Drive and East Lakeshore Drive.

Zippin' Jalapeño Poppers

½ (8-ounce) package cream cheese, softened
½ cup shredded Cheddar cheese
4 green onions, chopped
12 jalapeño peppers, halved lengthwise, seeds and membranes removed
12 slices bacon

Preheat oven to 400°. In a bowl, mix cream cheese, Cheddar cheese and onions together until evenly blended. Fill each jalapeño half with cheese mixture; put halves back together. Wrap each stuffed pepper with bacon slice; arrange bacon-wrapped peppers on foil-lined baking sheet. Bake 15 minutes or until bacon is crispy.

American Obstacle

American Obstacle

7859 South Route 37 • Kinmundy, IL 62854

217-690-3367 • www.americanobstacle.com • Find us on Facebook

Just off Interstate 57 (exit 127), find adventure tucked in the beautiful woods of Kinmundy. American Obstacle offers ziplines, rock climbing, outdoor tactical laser tag, kayaking, and team building. Come alone or bring a group and enjoy the outdoors with guides that are trained for fun and certified in safety. Visit their website, Facebook page, or call for more details on how to sign up. See you soon at American Obstacle.

April 1st–Mid-November: Weekends Only
Mid-May–Mid-August: Thursday–Monday
Tours at 10:00 am, Noon, 2:00 pm, 4:00 pm

"Heart Attack On A Plate"

3 large Idaho potatoes
Vegetable oil
1½ cups chopped and cooked bacon
2 cups melted cheese (American, nacho or Velveeta)

Wash and spiral slice potatoes; pat dry. Using a deep-fat fryer, heat oil to 325°; gently submerge potatoes. Wait until potatoes start to cook before trying to move them around (potatoes will stick to utensil if they are too raw). When they start to get a light golden brown color, use metal tongs to move them in the oil so they cook evenly. When they achieve the color you desire, pull out of fryer into a strainer basket to remove excess oil. Place a plate on top of strainer; flip over to achieve a round shape. Drizzle hot cheese over potatoes; top off with bacon. Serve with a smile!

Genoa Italian Concessions
Lincoln Heritage Festival

grab your fork

Lincoln Highway Heritage Festival

3rd Weekend in August

Downtown • Rochelle, IL 61068
815-562-6667 • www.lhhfest.com

If you enjoy family fun, car shows, parades, good food, and great entertainment the Lincoln Highway Heritage Festival is the place for your family to be. Celebrating more than 20 years of providing a safe environment and fun things to see and do should be at the top of your list. We will have a parade, pancakes in the park, carnival rides, business and direct sales booths, arts and crafts booths, and of course food booths. Enjoy three fun-filled days of the family doing just what they like to do. Don't forget we have some of the best entertainment around. Be sure to pick up your raffle tickets, surely your name will be drawn for some of the many items that have been donated for the festival. See you there.

Black Raspberry Brie

1 wheel Brie
1 cup Pheasant Hollow Raspberry Finale
1 tablespoon sugar
½ cup chopped walnuts
Flat bread cut into thin slices, toasted

Preheat oven to 400 °. In a small cast-iron skillet, put Brie in oven. In a saucepan over medium heat, cook Raspberry Finale until reduced by two thirds; add sugar. Pour over Brie; add walnuts. When Brie starts to soften, remove from oven. Serve with toasted flat bread.

Denny Franklin, Winemaker
Pheasant Hollow Winery

Pheasant Hollow Winery

14931 State Highway 37 • Whittington, IL 62897
618-629-2302 • www.pheasanthollowwinery.com • Find us on Facebook

The goal of Pheasant Hollow Winery is to make everyone that comes in the door feel comfortable and like part of the family. They support Illinois fruit growers by using locally grown fruit as much as possible. While making lots of fine grape wines, their strong suit is in the (non-grape) fruit wine market. The number one seller, Black and Blue Wine, is an excellent dessert wine that even pairs well with apple pie. Pheasant Hollow is able to ferment, press, and bottle wines throughout the year. There is always plenty of action in the cellars around the winery nestled on the eastern shore of Rend Lake in the scenic woodlands of southern Illinois. Come taste some of the finest wines of Illinois while enjoying the grand views of the surrounding area. Pheasant Hollow Winery has been growing the business and bottling wine for more than eighteen years.

Party Cheese Ball

1 (8-ounce) package Marcoot Jersey Creamery Plain or Garlic Herb Quark
1 (8-ounce) package cream cheese, softened
2 cups shredded Marcoot Jersey Creamery Cheddar cheese
1 tablespoon chopped pimento
1 tablespoon chopped green bell pepper
1 tablespoon chopped onion
2 tablespoons Worcestershire sauce
1 tablespoon lemon juice
¼ teaspoon salt
½ cup chopped pecans, optional

In a large bowl, combine Quark, cream cheese and Cheddar cheese using your hands to mix together. Add pimento, green pepper, onion, Worcestershire, lemon juice and salt; mix thoroughly. Shape into a ball. Spread pecans onto a plate; roll cheese ball in pecans until evenly coated. Refrigerate overnight before serving.

Marcoot Jersey Creamery

Mexi-Dip

1 pound ground beef
1 pound sausage
1 (16-ounce) package Velveeta cheese, cut into chunks
1 (10-ounce) can Rotel tomatoes with chiles
1 (15-ounce) can Hormel chili with beans
1 (4-ounce) can diced jalepeño peppers

In a skillet, brown meats until done; drain. Add to slow-cooker; with remaining ingredients. Cook on high until cheese melts; stir well. Turn to low until ready to serve.

Timber Ridge Outpost & Cabins

Sweet Corn Salsa

2 (15-ounce) cans Del Monte whole-kernel corn
1 (15-ounce) can black beans
1 (10-ounce) can Rotel tomatoes, drained
1 (8-ounce) can tomato sauce
Juice of 1 lime
1 avocado, chopped
½ jalapeño, chopped
½ Rio Grande pepper, chopped
Pinch salt

Mix all ingredients; serve with tortilla chips.

Mendota Sweet Corn Festival

Salsa with Balsamic Vinegar

Sweet, hot, tangy summer in a bowl.

1½ cups peeled, pitted and diced peaches
1 teaspoon minced fresh jalapeño
1 teaspoon chopped fresh cilantro
1 small shallot, minced
1 tablespoon Peach Balsamic Vinegar (available at The Tea Tree)
2 teaspoons lime zest

Combine all ingredients in a small bowl and stir.

Batavia Main Street

Batavia Farmer's Market and the Indoor Market

Farmer's Market: 1 North River Street • Batavia, IL 60510
Indoor Market: 15 East Wilson Street • Batavia, IL 60510
630-761-3528 • www.downtownbatavia.com

More than twenty-two years after its opening, the Farmer's Market continues in Batavian tradition, growing bigger and better each year. Patrons enjoy more than twenty-five vendors, each offering a variety of fresh vegetables, fruit, eggs, meat, cheese, herbs, flowers, breads, and more. The historic River Street, styled after a European woonerf, transforms into a community rendezvous that comes to life as live music fills the air. This is the place to be every Saturday morning. The indoor Italian-style Market at Gaetano's is River Street's perfect complement. Here, shoppers can find house-made aged meats and pastas as well as partially prepared meals to take home and wow family and friends. Third Saturdays feature the Artisan Collective, where visitors can enjoy living and shopping local. Browse handmade items from featured artists and designers. Join Batavia United Way and friends at Batavia Kiwanis for exciting kids' activities every week.

Farmer's Market
June–October • Saturdays: 8:00 am to Noon
Indoor Market
November–May • Saturdays: 9:00 am to Noon

Hostess Dip

1 (8-ounce) package cream cheese, softened
3 tablespoons milk
2 tablespoons lemon juice
1 teaspoon Worcestershire sauce
1 tablespoon mayonnaise
1 teaspoon mustard
¼ teaspoon ground horseradish sauce
¼ teaspoon garlic salt
½ teaspoon paprika
Corn chips

Combine all ingredients except corn chips. Mix well and chill
30 minutes. Pour into serving bowl and enjoy with corn chips.

Belvedere Mansion and Gardens

"The Crown Jewel of Galena"

1008 Park Avenue • Galena, IL 61036
815-777-0747 • www.belvederemansionandgardens.com

Often called "The Crown Jewel of Galena," Belvedere Mansion and Gardens is considered to be one of the finest Italianate mansions. With twenty-two lavishly decorated rooms and a history going back over 150 years, Belvedere attracts a lot of attention. Featuring the green drapes from the classic film *Gone with the Wind* and ornate furnishings from the estate of Liberace, everyone will find something amazing inside. The mansion was originally built in 1857 at a cost of $30,000.00 by Joseph Russel Jones, a United States Marshall to Congress and millionaire before the age of thirty. Today it is a private residence, but visitors may tour the mansion from May through November. Be sure to visit the gardens, designed by Danny Dinatale.

Dill Dip in a Rye Bowl

2 (8-ounce) packages cream cheese, softened
2 cups Hellman's mayonnaise
4 teaspoons parsley flakes
2¾ teaspoons dill weed
2 heaping teaspoons Lawry's seasoned salt
8 to 10 green onions, chopped
1 small plain Jarosch Bakery rye bread
Veggies for dipping (cucumbers, peppers, mushrooms, celery, carrots, etc.)

Combine all ingredients except bread and veggies; chill. Chop veggies into ideal dipping sized pieces. With a serrated knife, cut an oval around the top of the bread to hollow it out. Cut removed rye bread into cubes for dipping. Fill the hollowed loaf with Dill Dip and serve!

Jarosch Bakery

Jarosch Bakery

35 Arlington Heights Road • Elk Grove Village, IL 60007
847-437-1234 • www.jaroschbakery.com • Find us on Facebook

Jarosch Bakery is a third-generation, family-owned scratch bakery nestled in Elk Grove Village, a northwestern suburb of Chicago. From beautifully decorated cakes to decadent donuts, the Jaroschs have crafted high-quality breads and desserts for nearly sixty years. The bakery can trace its roots all the way back to Giessmannsdorf, Germany, where its founder, George Jarosch, began his baking career. George and his family emigrated to Chicago where his son, Herb, worked in a couple bakeries and even served in the Korean War as a baker before the father and son team opened Jarosch Bakery in October 1959.

Over the years, as the business grew, the bakery experienced several production area expansions. In 1989, Ken Jarosch, Herb's son, and his wife Kathy joined the bakery. Today they continue to ensure Jarosch Bakery provides northwest Chicagoland with freshly made custom cakes, breads, pastries, cookies, donuts, and coffeecakes.

Monday–Friday: 6:30 am to 6:30 pm
Saturday: 6:30 am to 5:00 pm

Birdie Buffet

All God's creatures must eat to survive. Here's a good bird buffet to provide for our feathered friends.

Unsalted peanuts
Black oil sunflower seeds
Black niger
Grape jelly
Oranges
Nectar

A simple way to start attracting birds to your dinner party is to place food where they can find it. Some birds choose to dine up high on a tree branch, others enjoy their meal on a mesh or platform bird feeder, and some will even swoop to the ground to discover a special treat. Set your table with separate delightful dishes for a variety of bird species to enjoy. Unsalted peanuts, for example, will attract blue jays. A spread of black oil sunflower seeds added to your smorgasbord will attract a diverse and colorful crowd of woodpeckers, cardinals, nuthatches and many migrating sparrows. To entice a visit from goldfinches, add some black niger, an oily seed that makes an excellent source of protein and energy for our feathered friends; however don't let it dry out or the birds won't eat it. Interested in attracting orioles? Spread some grape jelly on your feeder, or slice and dice fresh oranges. Be the perfect hostess and provide a fresh water source to wash down all the delicious food. To lure a hummingbird, offer an appealing and delightful drink from a nectar feeder. A natural recipe consists of 1 part sugar and 4 parts water with no food coloring.

Hickory Knolls Discovery Center

Hickory Knolls Discovery Center

A facility of the St. Charles Park • James O. Breen Community Park

3795 Campton Hills Road • St. Charles, IL 60175
630-513-4399 • www.stcnature.org

Nestled at the edge of 130 acres of oak woodlands, wetlands, and prairies, the Hickory Knolls Discovery Center offers a unique blend of rustic nature and contemporary comforts. The LEED-certified building features beautiful views and an open floor plan with rental and programming space. Live animal displays, including state-endangered Blanding's turtles, offer guests up close interaction with reptiles native to Illinois. Nature programs for all ages, birthday parties, and special events provide guests with many educational and social opportunities to connect to our local environment. Visit this premiere environmental discovery center in the Fox Valley today! Free admission.

Tuesday–Saturday: 10:00 am to 4:00 pm
Sunday: Noon to 4:00 pm

Smoky Pretzel Mix

½ stick butter, melted
3 tablespoons brown sugar
1 teaspoon smoked paprika
¾ teaspoon cayenne
3 cups mini pretzels
2 cups mixed nuts

Preheat oven to 325°. In a bowl, combine butter, sugar, paprika and cayenne; mix well. Pour over pretzels and nuts; toss until evenly covered. Spread mixture on baking sheet; bake 10 minutes. Stir with a spatula; bake another 10 minutes. Remove from heat; cool completely.

Marlene Pennekamp
Cahokia Mounds Museum Society Member

Bread & Breakfast

Fearless Food Gardening Cornbread Muffins with Poblano Peppers

Cornbread ranks high on our list of comfort foods. We like to mix in some sweet corn and peppers for added flavor and texture. Poblanos give a touch of heat. If you want to turn it up a notch, substitute serranos or jalapeños.

1 ear fresh sweet corn
1 cup all-purpose flour
1 cup medium-grind yellow cornmeal
3 teaspoons baking powder
½ teaspoon salt
5 tablespoons butter, softened
2 tablespoons sugar
1 egg, beaten
1 cup milk
½ poblano pepper, finely chopped (about ½ cup)

Preheat oven to 400°. While oven is preheating, cook unhusked corn in microwave 3 to 4 minutes. Remove corn from microwave and place on cutting board. Cut bottom inch off, then shake to release cob from husk; run cob under cold water or set aside to cool. In a large bowl, combine flour, cornmeal, baking powder and salt; stir well. In a separate bowl, combine butter and sugar; add egg and milk and stir well. Pour liquid mixture over flour mixture and stir until lumpy. Position corn on cutting board, cut side down; start at the top and saw downward to remove kernels from ear. Fold corn and pepper into muffin batter until just combined; do not overmix. Spoon batter into 12-cup nonstick muffin pan. Bake 20 to 25 minutes, until golden and cracked on top. Makes 12 muffins.

Chicago Flower & Garden Show

CHICAGO FLOWER & GARDEN SHOW

March

Navy Pier • 600 East Grand Avenue • Chicago, IL 60611
312-241-1250 • www.chicagoflower.com

The roots of the Chicago Flower & Garden show can be traced back as far as 1847. When it first began, the show was a flower and fruit exposition presented by the Chicago Horticultural Society (CHS). Similar to today, the events were organized by like-minded gardeners who were looking for a way to trade horticulture tips and techniques among exhibitors and participants. Today, 170 years later, the show welcomes more than 40,000 attendees to the Festival Halls in Navy Pier where they can experience every facet of horticulture. While visiting, attendees can walk through life-sized gardens, participate in DIY workshops, learn from educational seminars, enjoy garden-to-table cooking presentations, and more!

Pizza Dough

1 teaspoon dry active yeast
1½ cups warm water, divided
4 cups flour (all-purpose or bread flour), plus more for rolling dough
1 teaspoon salt
¼ cup olive oil, plus more for drizzling

Add yeast to a small bowl; add ½ cup warm water (between 80° and 100°). Stir lightly with a spoon; set aside 5 minutes for yeast to activate. (You'll be able to smell it.) In a mixing bowl, add flour, salt, remaining 1 cup water and yeast mixture. If you have a mixer, use dough hook and set to a medium speed. Mix until all the liquid is absorbed by flour. Add olive oil and continue mixing 3 to 4 minutes or until you get a good bread dough consistency. Place a handful of flour on a flat surface; dust your hands. Place dough onto flour and knead vigorously 8 to 10 minutes or until texture is smooth and uniform. If dough seems a little sticky, add a little more flour. One method to knead is to lean on dough with the palm of your hand. Press dough to mixing surface. Fold dough and repeat. After kneading, place dough in a bowl; drizzle with just enough olive oil to cover top of dough. Cover bowl with cloth; set in warm area. Let dough rise an hour; punch down. Wait another 30 to 45 minutes; dough is now ready to ferment. Place in refrigerator 16 to 28 hours. Remove from refrigerator and warm to room temperature. Dust a rolling pin with flour; roll out dough on floured surface until desired shape. If you think you can, forget the rolling pin and try stretching it out by hand.

Chicago Pizza Tours

Chicago Pizza Tours

Chicago, IL 60606

888-210-3237 • www.chicagopizzatours.com

Chicago Pizza Tours delivers bus-guided food tours of pizzerias significant to the culture of Chicago's renowned pizza scene. Guests are given the opportunity to feel like a local as they dine off the beaten path in unique neighborhoods. As you savor a variety of pizza, you'll learn all about the science of ingredient selection as well as the baking methods that make these pizzas so delicious. Designed by Jonathan Porter, the tours meet in a central part of the downtown Chicago area and travel approximately 15 to 20 miles through various neighborhoods to give guests a chance to experience pizzerias they may not explore on their own. Every tour visits four restaurants, each serving a drastically different tasting slice that will make it difficult to choose a favorite. Rather than finding the best slice, it is about the journey.

Daily: 8:00 am to 8:00 pm

Popovers Romanoff

Popovers:

2 cups flour
6 large eggs
2 cups 2% milk
1 teaspoon salt
6 tablespoons melted butter
Strawberries, sliced

Preheat oven to 375°. Heat popover pan in oven while it preheats. In a blender, combine flour, eggs, milk, salt and butter; mix well. Grease 12 popover tins with cooking spray; fill a little over half full with batter. Bake 40 minutes; do not open oven. Pierce each popover with fork or paring knife to let steam escape; bake an additional 5 to 8 minutes. Cool slightly. Place each popover on a plate; slice in half. Layer with Sauce (below) and sliced strawberries.

Sauce:

1½ cups sour cream
2 tablespoons powdered sugar
2 tablespoons brown sugar
½ teaspoon cinnamon
¼ teaspoon nutmeg
1 tablespoon rum or brandy
1 teaspoon grated orange peel

In a bowl, combine sour cream, sugars, cinnamon, nutmeg, rum or brandy and orange peel. Mix well; chill overnight to blend flavors.

The Steamboat House Bed and Breakfast, Galena

The Steamboat House
Bed & Breakfast

605 South Prospect Street • Galena, IL 61036
815-777-2317 • www.thesteamboathouse.com

The Steamboat House is a historic, Gothic Revival mansion built in 1855 for Daniel Smith Harris and his wife Sarah. Harris was a famous steamboat captain and one of the first settlers in Galena. Sarah was a botanist, suffragette, and one of the first female physicians in Illinois. The mansion was also a stop on the Underground Railroad. This grand, 7,000-square-foot inn offers privacy in the form of five spacious and beautifully appointed guestrooms, cozy parlors, a wraparound

front porch, and screened garden gazebo. Filled with natural light, our spacious guestrooms have fireplaces and private baths, LCD TVs, DVD players, and fine linens. Social opportunities are offered in the billiard room, library, and huge formal dining room. Private, off-street guest parking and covered motorcycle/antique car parking is provided.

Violet Jelly

1 quart common blue violet blossoms
3½ cups boiling water
1 lemon, juiced
1 (1.75- ounce) package powdered pectin
4 cups sugar

Rinse blossoms in cold water; drain. Put in a glass jar or bowl; cover with boiling water. Cover container; let stand 24 hours. Strain the blue infusion; discard violet blossoms. In a saucepan, combine lemon juice, 3 cups blue infusion and pectin; bring to a boil. Add sugar. Bring back to a boil; boil hard 1 minute. Remove from heat; skim foam off the top. Pour into sterilized glass jars; seal. Place jars in a pan; add water three quarters of the way to top of jar. Bring to a boil; boil 5 minutes to ensure a proper seal.

Black Hawk State Historic Site

Black Hawk State Historic Site

1510 46th Avenue • Rock Island, IL 61201
Museum: 309-788-9536 • Office: 309-788-0177
www.blackhawkpark.org

This wooded, steeply rolling, 208-acre tract bordering the Rock River is identified with the Sauk nation and the warrior Black Hawk. This was the westernmost battle of the Revolutionary War. In 1927 John Hauberg was key to the creation of a state park. From 1933 to 1935 the Civilian Conservation Corps built hiking trails, two picnic shelters, and much of the present-day Watch Tower Lodge. An exhibit about the CCC is found in the lodge which houses the Hauberg Museum featuring full-size replicas of Sauk winter and summer houses and dioramas featuring activities of the Sauk and Meskwaki typical of the period 1750 to 1830. The illustrated book *Twelve Moons: A Year with the Sauk and Meskwaki, 1817–1818* is available at the museum. The lodge's large main room—with two massive stone fireplaces and original woodwork—is popular for wedding receptions. In 1972, Citizens to Preserve Black Hawk Park Foundation was formed for support. In 1979 the Park became a State Historic Site. In 1984 the north forest was declared a nature preserve.

Site Grounds: Daily Dawn to Dusk
Museum:
March to October
Wednesday–Sunday: 9:00 am to 5:00 pm
November to February
Wednesday–Sunday: 9:00 am to 4:00 pm

Hotel Custer Coffee Cake

This historic recipe was a specialty at the coffee shop at Galesburg's Hotel Custer. Innkeeper's has revived this ultimate comfort coffeecake and serves it regularly.

3 sticks butter, divided
4 tablespoons cinnamon
3 cups plus 4 tablespoons flour, divided
2 cups packed brown sugar
2 cups chopped pecans
3 teaspoons baking powder
1 teaspoon salt
1½ cups sugar
2 eggs
1 cup milk
2 teaspoons vanilla

Melt 1 stick butter; place in a bowl. Add cinnamon, 4 tablespoons flour, brown sugar and pecans; mix by hand. Set aside to use for topping. Preheat oven to 350°. Butter and flour a 9x13-inch pan; set aside. Place remaining flour, baking powder, salt and sugar in a food processor. Cut remaining butter into 8 pats each stick; add 4 pats to processor and process in short 15 second bursts. Repeat until all butter is added and mixture is consistency of cornmeal. Beat eggs with milk in a bowl large enough to hold flour mixture. Mix together flour and egg mixtures by hand. Add vanilla; mix just enough to combine, being careful not to overmix. Pour half of batter in pan, spreading to all sides; top with half of topping. Repeat layering, beginning with remaining batter, finishing with remaining topping. Bake 30 minutes or until golden brown.

Innkeeper's Fresh Roasted Coffee

Innkeeper's Fresh Roasted Coffee

80 North Seminary Street • Galesburg, IL 61401
309-344-2625 • www.innkeepers-coffee.com • Find us on Facebook

Experience the world of specialty coffee at Innkeeper's Fresh Roasted Coffee in Galesburg. You may buy fresh-roasted beans or savor a drink from the espresso bar or drive through. Breakfast and lunch are served, including house-baked pastries, desserts, and chocolate truffles. Innkeeper's is a locally owned and operated roastery committed to offering you the finest, freshest, most flavorful and aromatic coffee available: the best stolen moment of your day. All of the coffees are the highest grade of Arabica beans from small plantations. They only roast shade-grown coffees that are environmentally friendly. All of the beans are either single-origin or estate coffees, including the beans of Innkeeper's signature blends. Their small batch, artisan roasting guarantees freshness. In addition to single bean roasts, their specialty roasts and blends have been developed with great care to ensure you experience the aroma and flavor of each coffee variety. The flavored coffees are also hand-roasted using the highest quality beans.

Monday–Friday: 6:30 am to 6:00 pm
Saturday: 7:00 am to 5:00 pm
Sunday: 8:00 am to 5:00 pm

Cinnamon Coffee Cake

Cake:

1½ cups sifted flour
2½ teaspoons baking powder
½ cup sugar
1 egg white
¼ cup oil
¾ cup skim milk

Preheat oven to 375°. Sift together flour, baking powder and sugar. Blend in egg white, oil and milk; stir until flour is moistened. Set aside.

Topping:

½ cup brown sugar
2 tablespoons flour
2 tablespoons oil
2 tablespoons cinnamon

In another bowl, make topping by mixing together sugar, flour, oil and cinnamon. Spread half of batter in an oiled 8-inch square pan; sprinkle with half of topping. Add remaining batter; sprinkle with rest of topping. Bake 30 minutes or until done. Yield: 9 servings.

Long Hollow Canopy Tours

Long Hollow Canopy Tours

3247 West Longhollow Road • Galena, IL 61028
815-281-2853 • www.longhollowcanopytours.com

Let your feet fly, your mind wander, and your smile shine on this exciting zipline adventure. Immerse yourself in the gorgeous hardwoods of northwestern Illinois for approximately two and a half hours on this fully guided tour. The course includes Ground School, UTV ride, six ziplines, rappel, a scenic hike, sky bridge, and quick jump. Reach speeds up to forty mph and heights of seventy-five feet! Finish the tour with an adrenaline rushing 1,230-foot zip. This exhilarating and breathtaking tour is open to participants ten years old and older weighing between 70 to 250 pounds. The adventure lasts today but the memory lasts a lifetime.

April–November
9:00 am to 5:00 pm

Oatmeal Muffins

1 stick butter, softened
½ cup sugar
2 eggs, beaten
¾ cup crushed pineapple, drained
1 cup oatmeal
¾ cup all-purpose flour
2 teaspoons baking powder
½ tablespoon cinnamon or to taste
2 cups blueberries (or cranberries)

Preheat oven to 350°. In a mixing bowl, cream butter and sugar; mix in eggs and pineapple. Stir in oatmeal, flour, baking powder and cinnamon; fold in fruit. Put in lined cupcake pans; bake 20 minutes.

Green Tree Inn Bed & Breakfast, Elsah, IL

Visit Alton

200 Piasa Street • Alton, IL 62002
618-465-6676 • www.VisitAlton.com

Adventure awaits all around Alton, Illinois, where three great rivers come together creating a getaway spot like no other. From hiking and biking along the Mighty Mississippi, to exploring the river's strength at its largest locks and dam, to beginning the "Voyage of Discovery with Lewis & Clark," there is no end to the history, outdoor activities, and excitement available throughout the charming river communities stretched along one of the most scenic byways in the United States. Relax and sip local wines beside the Mississippi River at Grafton Winery and Brewhaus. Rise 150 feet in the air at the Lewis and Clark Confluence Tower and see the confluence of the Missouri and Mississippi rivers. See all of that and much, much more by requesting a travel guide at www.VisitAlton.com.

Monday–Friday: 8:30 am to 5:00 pm
Saturday & Sunday: 9:00 am to 3:00 pm

Ms. Ella's Petite Poppy Seed Scones

2 cups all-purpose flour
½ cup sugar
2½ tablespoons poppy seeds
2 teaspoons baking powder
1 teaspoon baking soda
½ teaspoon salt
6 tablespoons cold unsalted butter, diced into ¼ -inch cubes
½ cup plus 2 tablespoons heavy cream, divided
1½ tablespoons lemon zest
3½ tablespoons lemon juice, divided
¼ teaspoon lemon extract
Few drops yellow food coloring
1 large egg
1 cup powdered sugar

Preheat oven to 400°. Line a baking sheet with parchment paper or silicone liner; set aside. In a mixing bowl, whisk together flour, sugar, poppy seeds, baking powder, baking soda and salt. Cut butter into flour mixture using a pastry cutter or 2 knives until it resembles coarse meal. Make a well in center of mixture; chill while preparing cream mixture. In a small mixing bowl, whisk together ½ cup plus 1 tablespoon cream, lemon zest, 1½ tablespoons lemon juice, lemon extract, food coloring and egg until well combined. Add cream mixture to well in flour mixture. Stir using a spatula until it starts to come together; gently roll mixture by hand several times until it has come together well (careful not to overwork dough or scones won't be tender). Pour mixture onto floured surface; dust top lightly with flour. Gently pat and shape dough into a 7x7-inch square. Cut into 9 equal squares; cut each square in half on diagonal to create 2 triangles. Transfer to baking sheet, spacing scones evenly apart; brush tops lightly with remaining cream. Bake 10 to 14 minutes until set. Transfer to a wire rack, cool slightly. In a small bowl, combine powdered sugar with 2 tablespoons lemon juice; stir until smooth. Spoon glaze over tops to edges. Allow glaze to set at room temperature until glaze slightly hardens. Store in an air-tight container.

Historic Hull House Inn

Historic Hull House Inn

1517 Walnut Street • Murphysboro, IL 62966
618-305-5625 • www.historichullhouseinn.com

The Historic Hull House is an Italianate Victorian home that was added to the National Register of Historic Places in 2006. The decor throughout the house is along the lines of Victorian Farmhouse, departing from the usually frilly nature one associates with a Victorian-era inn. Instead it's decorated with a zen-like eclecticism. One thing you will not find on the premises is a television. There is WiFi, so tablets and phones work perfectly. The Hull House Inn is about relaxation. It's the perfect place to unplug from daily life, read a book, or have a conversation. We are conveniently located approximately twelve miles from the local wine trails and walking distance from the quaint shops in downtown Murphysboro.

Images courtesy of *The Southern Illinoian/Life & Style* in Southern Illinois

Cinnamon Roll Bread

2 cups all-purpose flour
1 tablespoon baking powder
½ teaspoon salt
½ cup plus ⅓ cup sugar, divided
1 egg, room temperature, lightly beaten
1 cup milk
2 teaspoons vanilla extract

⅓ cup plain Greek yogurt
  (or sour cream)
2 teaspoons cinnamon
2 tablespoons water
½ cup powdered sugar
1 tablespoon milk

Preheat oven to 350°. Spray 5x9-inch loaf pan with nonstick cooking spray. In a large bowl, combine flour, baking powder, salt and ½ cup sugar. In a small bowl, combine egg, milk, vanilla and yogurt. Add dry ingredients into wet; stir to combine (if desired, mix with large wooden spoon as no mixer is required). Add dough to loaf pan; set aside. In a small bowl, swirl together remaining sugar, cinnamon and water; using a tablespoon, drop spoonfuls of this mixture over dough. Using a knife, make swirl designs in dough to incorporate cinnamon mixture. Bake 45 to 50 minutes or until toothpick inserted into center comes out clean. Remove bread from oven; transfer to a cooling rack. Cool 15 minutes; remove bread from pan and allow to cool completely. Stir together powdered sugar and milk to make glaze. Pour over top of bread and enjoy.

Pekin Park District

Pekin Park District

1701 Court Street • Pekin, IL 61554
309-347-7275 • www.pekinparkdistrict.org

The Pekin Park District has been serving the community of Pekin, home of Senator Everett McKinley Dirksen, since 1902 and is your place for summer and winter family fun! While visiting in the warmer months, play a round of golf at the four-star-rated Lick Creek Golf Course and check out DragonLand Water Park to swim, slide, and splash around. Play Magic Dragon Mini Golf and then walk over to the Pekin Lagoon where you can take a beautiful paddle boat ride. Or stop by McNaughton Park and enjoy an adventurous hike on Potawatomi Trail, go on a guided horseback ride, or fish in one of two lakes. For the extreme bike enthusiast, ride the trails through Dirksen and Independence Parks. When the weather gets cold, the Pekin Park District invites you indoors to skate on the ice at Veteran's Memorial Arena. Call for hours and information.

Pumpkin Bread

1 cup sugar
1 cup oil
1 teaspoon nutmeg
1 teaspoon cinnamon
1½ teaspoons salt
4 eggs, beaten
1 cup pumpkin purée
⅔ cup water
2 teaspoons baking soda
3 cups flour

Preheat oven to 350°. Grease and flour 2 (5x9-inch) loaf pans; set aside. In a large bowl, mix all ingredients; pour batter evenly in loaf pans. Bake 1 hour; cool in pans 10 minutes. Remove cakes from pans; finish cooling on racks. Wrap in foil and store in refrigerator until ready to serve.

The Wildlife Discovery Center

1401 Middlefork • Lake Forest, IL 60045

847-810-3663 • www.wildlifediscoverycenter.org • Find us on Facebook

The Wildlife Discovery Center (WDC) is a living natural history museum and one of the region's unique hidden gems. It is a place of learning and wonder, where people of all ages can explore the important concepts of wildlife conservation and environmental stewardship in an intimate setting. The learning journey brings visitors face-to-face with a variety of reptiles, amphibians, birds, and mammals. There are also interpretive trails and nature-based programs for all to enjoy. Their mission is to motivate all generations to come to know, respect, and protect the challenged and often endangered ecosystems with a focus on their wildlife.

Tuesday, Friday–Sunday: 10:00 am to 4:00 pm

Banana Bread

1 cup butter, softened
1 cup margarine, softened
4 cups sugar
8 eggs
8 cups mashed bananas (16 to 20 bananas)
6 cups all-purpose flour
4 teaspoons baking powder
4 teaspoons baking soda

Preheat oven to 350°. Lightly grease 4 loaf pans; set aside. Cream together butter and margarine in a stand mixer; scrape paddle and bowl. Add sugar and beat; scrape paddle and bowl. Add eggs and beat; scrape paddle and bowl. Add mashed bananas and beat; scrape paddle and bowl. Add remaining ingredients and beat until well mixed. Pour batter into treated loaf pans. Bake about 50 minutes or until a toothpick inserted in center comes out clean. Makes 4 loaves or 12 mini loaves.

Sweet Dream Desserts & Catering

Sweet Dream
Desserts & Catering

1969B DeKalb Avenue • Sycamore, IL 60178
www.sweetdreamdesserts.com • Find us on Facebook

Sweet Dream Desserts & Catering is a friendly, small-town bakery and catering service famous for delicious, center-filled cupcakes unlike anything you'll find in those expensive cafés in Chicago's trendy neighborhoods. Plus, they're close enough that you can come back for more anytime. Not just a cupcake joint, Sycamore native and owner Deanna Watkins opens the doors each morning to serve continental-style breakfast fare, such as scones and sweet breads, while her husband, Chef Phil, prepares the day's catering orders. They also boast a variety of homemade cookies just like grandma used to make, plus other desserts. Full-sized cakes and cheesecakes are available for any occasion— from baby showers to birthdays and weddings. Can't stop in for a bite? Let Chef Phil cater to you. From a simple, summer BBQ to an elegant, plated meal, Sweet Dream Desserts & Catering has a full menu of meal options to satisfy your taste and budget. From appetizers to soup, dinner, and dessert, they've got you covered. "Let us make your ordinary day a sweet dream and your dreams a sweet memory."

Monday–Friday: 8:00 am to 6:00 pm
Saturday: 8:00 am to 3:00 pm
Sunday: Catering only

Old German Pancakes

This is the Tanner children's favorite breakfast.

1 cup milk
¾ cup sifted flour
Pinch salt
2 teaspoons sugar
3 eggs, beaten
½ cup butter, melted
Powdered sugar

In a bowl, beat milk, flour, salt and sugar with a whisk until smooth; add eggs and blend. Gradually add butter, mixing well. Warm skillet, add ¼ to ⅓ cup batter; tip pan from side to side covering the whole pan with a thin layer. When crisp around edges and browned underneath, lift pancake with a spatula, flipping to brown on the other side. Transfer to warm platter or plate; fill with fruit filling, cream cheese or syrup if desired. Roll pancake up and sprinkle outside with powdered sugar.

Tanners Orchard

Tanners Orchard

740 State Route 40 • Speer, IL 61479
309-493-5442 • www.tannersorchard.com
www.facebook.com/tannersappleorchard

Since 1947, four generations of the Tanner family have welcomed visitors to an amazing country farm experience. At Tanners Orchard, you'll find a family atmosphere where fun is the order of the day. More than 11,000 trees and seventeen varieties of apples grow in the orchard, and more than twenty acres of pumpkins are grown along with various other fruits and vegetables. You'll enjoy perusing the fruits and vegetables for sale in the farmers market along with a large assortment of gourmet foods, home décor, and gifts. The Apple Bin Bakery and Café offers delicious lunch and dinner options, the Tanners' signature homemade caramel apples, and apple cider donuts. The Back 40 Fun Acres, corn maze, and farm animals will keep you and your family busy for the day. Tanners Orchard is the perfect place to start your own family tradition.

August and November
Monday–Saturday: 8:00 am to 5:00 pm
September and October
Daily: 8:00 am to 8:00 pm

Danish Æbleskiver (Danish Pancakes)

2 cups flour
2 teaspoons baking powder
1 teaspoon salt
2 teaspoons sugar
2 cups milk
4 eggs, separated
2 tablespoons margarine, softened
½ teaspoon lemon extract
Vegetable oil
Powdered sugar
Strawberry jam or jelly

In a bowl, sift dry ingredients. In another bowl, beat milk, egg yolks, margarine and lemon extract together; mix into dry ingredients. Beat eggs whites in a bowl; fold into flour-milk mixture. Fry in æbleskiver pan prepared with vegetable oil in each cup; add oil as needed while cooking. Sprinkle with powdered sugar and serve with strawberry jam or jelly. Recipe makes about 40 pancakes.

Johannes Smits
Scandinavian Day Festival

Scandinavian Day Festival
Vasa Park

September

35W217 Route 31 • South Elgin, IL 60177
847-695-6720 • www.vasaparkil.com • www.scandinaviandayil.com

Scandinavian Park, Inc. NFP invites you to come celebrate the culture, heritage, and traditions of Denmark, Finland, Iceland, Norway, and Sweden at the tranquil, twenty-five-acre Vasa Park property situated on Route 31 along the beautiful Fox River in South Elgin. Vasa Park features towering, mature oak trees and wide open spaces. Scandinavian Park, Inc. NFP holds numerous community events throughout the year celebrating Scandinavian and Nordic traditions, including the big Scandinavian Day Festival on the second Sunday in September. A festive Midsommar Celebration is also held in June, and a delicious Fish Boil/ Harvest Festival takes place in the autumn. Events are open to the public and everyone is welcome. In addition, Vasa Park is available for outdoor rentals May through October with ample parking for over 1,000 cars. Vasa Park is the perfect setting for weddings, family reunions, company picnics, outdoor concerts, and festivals of all sizes.

Crêpes Suzette

6 tablespoons flour
6 eggs
6 tablespoons milk
3 tablespoons heavy cream
3 oranges
1 cup unsalted butter, softened, plus more for cooking
10 tablespoons sugar, divided
7 tablespoons Cointreau, divided
1 tablespoon kirsch
1 teaspoon orange flower water
5 tablespoons cognac

In a medium bowl, whisk flour and eggs; add milk and cream, whisking until smooth. Pour batter through a fine strainer into a sealable bowl; cover and refrigerate at least 2 hours or overnight. Using a vegetable peeler, remove rind from 2 oranges, avoiding pith; mince rind and set aside. Juice oranges; set aside. In a medium bowl using an electric mixer, beat 1 cup butter with 8 tablespoons sugar on high speed 2 minutes or until light and fluffy. Add rind; beat 1 minute. Gradually drizzle in juice, 2 tablespoons Cointreau, kirsch and orange flower water, beating constantly 2 minutes or until very light and fluffy. Heat seasoned crêpe pan or small nonstick skillet over medium-high heat until hot; grease pan with a little butter. Pour in ¼ cup batter; working quickly, swirl batter to just coat pan. Cook 1 minute or until edges brown. Turn with a spatula; brown other side. Transfer to a plate; repeat with remaining batter, greasing pan only as needed. To serve, melt orange butter sauce in a 12-inch skillet over medium heat until bubbling. Dip both sides of 1 crêpe in sauce; with best side facing down, fold in half and then in half again. Repeat process with remaining crêpes, arranging and overlapping crêpes around perimeter of pan. Sprinkle with remaining sugar. Remove pan from heat; pour remaining Cointreau and cognac over crêpes. Carefully ignite with a match; spoon sauce over crêpes until flame dies out. Serve immediately.

3 French Hens

3 French Hens

123 West Illinois Avenue • Morris, IL 60450
815-513-5600 • www.3frenchhensmarket.blogspot.com • Find us on Facebook

"Part farmers' market, part high-end swap meet, this Euro-style, open-air emporium lies along the picturesque Illinois and Michigan canal. It features more than 130 vendors selling antique furniture, salvaged items, vintage housewares, and crafts, as well as baked goods, artisanal cheeses, flowers, and local produce." —Bob Vila™. The 3 French Hens market was named one of the top 5 markets in the nation by *Romantic Homes Magazine*.

May–October: 2nd Saturdays
November: 2nd Friday night and Saturday

French Toast

2 eggs, beaten
½ cup milk
1 teaspoon sugar
1 pinch salt
7 teaspoon light brown sugar, divided
1 teaspoon vanilla
⅛ teaspoon cinnamon, plus more for plating
6 (1-inch thick) slices French bread, cut on the diagonal
Melted butter
Shredded coconut
Powdered sugar
Warm syrup

Preheat oven to 250°. In a flat-bottom bowl, mix together eggs, milk, sugar, salt, 1 teaspoon light brown sugar, vanilla and cinnamon; soak each slice of bread in liquid mixture 15 seconds. In a buttered pan over medium heat, sear each slice to a golden brown. Place seared toast in a greased glass casserole dish; top each slice with 1 teaspoon light brown sugar. Drizzle a small amount melted butter over sugar, top with coconut. Bake 10 to 15 minutes. When plating, garnish bottom of plate with powdered sugar and cinnamon; plate toast. Sprinkle lightly with powdered sugar; serve with warm syrup.

Maple Leaf Cottage Inn

Bed and Breakfast
MAPLE LEAF COTTAGE INN
Est. 1949

Maple Leaf Cottage Inn

12 Selma Street • Elsah, IL 62028
618-374-1684 • www.MapleLeafCottageInn.com

Maple Leaf Cottage Inn is the perfect destination for overnight lodging or special occasions. The historic village of Elsah is nestled in the bluffs off the Great River Road. Whether you are looking for a quiet place to relax or a unique setting for that special occasion, Maple Leaf Cottage Inn will immerse you in Southern hospitality. You will enjoy the breathtaking scenic views or may choose to enjoy miles of trails either on foot or using the inn's complimentary bike rental. Just minutes away from fine dining, shopping, and entertainment in Alton and Grafton, Maple Leaf Cottage Inn is the perfect place for making memories that last a lifetime. Maple Leaf Cottage Inn is the winner of the Trip Advisor 2017 Certificate of Excellence Award and two-time winner of Best Overnight Stay—voted #1 by the People's Choice Award.

- Scenic getaway just fourty minutes from St. Louis
- Unique, private rooms with bath
- Delicious homemade breakfast included
- Minutes from fine dining and entertainment
- Complimentary bike rentals

VacationIdea
DREAM VACATION MAGAZINE
"Best Romantic Getaway"

lonely planet
We are featured in Lonely Planet's guidebook USA's Best Trips - 52 Amazing Road Trips

2017
CERTIFICATE of EXCELLENCE
tripadvisor

Sweet & Sassy Breakfast Bagel

1 Lender's onion bagel
2 tablespoons mango preserves
1 tablespoon butter
¼ cup chorizo sausage, casing removed
½ teaspoon minced jalapeño pepper
2 tablespoons chopped green onion
2 tablespoons chopped tomatoes
1 egg
¼ cup shredded Cheddar cheese

Split bagel and toast halves; spread preserves on both halves. In a small frying pan over medium-high heat, melt butter; cook sausage. Add pepper, onion and tomatoes; cook 1 minute. Break in egg to scramble; add cheese just before egg is fully cooked. Place scrambled mixture on 1 bagel half; top with other bagel half. Enjoy at the table or on the go.

Lender's Bagels

Mattoon Bagelfest at Peterson Park

3rd Week in July

500 Broadway Avenue • Mattoon, IL 61938
800-500-6286 • www.mattoonbagelfest.com • Find us on Facebook

ALL ABOARD FOR
BAGEL FEST

The story of Bagelfest is one of hospitality. In 1986, when the local Mattoon plant became the Lender's Bagel plant, brand owner Murray Lender knew he needed to introduce the Mattoon community to the bagel. It wasn't a common item in the homes of most people in Mattoon, so Murray hosted a free bagel breakfast to introduce the community and potential employees to what a Lender's bagel is all about. Tables were lined end to end down the middle of Broadway Avenue in downtown Mattoon. Young and old alike enjoyed the hospitality and the community spirit of the event. The breakfast inspired leaders in the community to make the free bagel breakfast into a full-scale community festival, and the Mattoon Bagelfest was born. Thirty-two years later, the event is still going strong with five days of fun, music, food, and, of course, the "Free Bagel Breakfast."

Apple Butter

8 pounds apples
3 cups apple cider
1 cup apple cider vinegar
3 cups white sugar
2¼ cups packed brown sugar
1 tablespoon ground cinnamon
2 teaspoons ground cloves
2 teaspoons ground nutmeg

Wash apples; remove stems, quarter and core. Using a large stockpot, cook slowly in cider and vinegar until fruit is soft. Press through a colander, food mill or strainer. Cook fruit pulp with sugars and spices 20 minutes, stirring frequently. Pour hot apple butter into hot half-pint or pint jars, leaving ¼-inch headspace. Wipe jar rims clean and adjust 2-piece canning lids. Process 5 minutes in a boiling water bath canner. Remove jars; allow to cool completely before checking seals. Label and date each jar. Store in a cool place away from direct sunlight for up to 1 year.

Rockome Garden Foods

127 North County Road 425 East • Arcola, IL 61910
217-268-4107 • www.rockomefoods.com

Since 2014, Sam and Sue Ellen Gingerich have owned and operated Rockome Garden Foods located in the heart of central Illinois Amish country. The store maintains the look and appeal of an authentic Amish general store offering a wide variety of "farm-to-table" ingredients and food products. You'll discover local honey, original recipe jams and jellies, home-canned fruits and vegetables, as well as unique relishes, spreads, and dips for snacking. A full-service deli offers the highest quality meats and cheeses and the on-site bakery tempts the senses with fresh baked breads, cinnamon rolls, donuts, and cookies. Old-fashaioned candy is also available, and custom-made gift boxes and baskets are available year round. Housed in the store is a milk pasteurization facility, producing grass-fed cow and goat milk and cheese. The store is a family endeavor with the six Gingerich children participating in making the store a "must see and visit" destination.

Monday–Saturday: 9:00 am to 5:00 pm

House Bacon Jam

3 pounds bacon, chopped
4 large Spanish onions, large dice
8 garlic cloves, smashed
1¼ cups cider vinegar
1 cup brown sugar
½ cup maple syrup
1¾ cups brewed coffee
1 teaspoon ground black pepper

In a heavy-bottomed saucepan, cook bacon over medium heat until browned. Remove bacon from pan, reserving 2 tablespoons bacon grease in bottom. Add onion; cook until softened. Add garlic; cook 1 minute. Add remaining ingredients and bacon; bring to a boil. Reduce heat to a simmer; simmer uncovered, stirring occasionally, 2½ hours or until syrupy. Transfer mixture to a blender; purée until spreadable. Refrigerate in labeled and dated container up to 1 month.

Eric Chaplin, Sous Chef
Le Jardin at Cantigny Park

The First Division Museum at Cantigny Park

Cantigny Golf

CANTIGNY PARK | GARDENS MUSEUMS GOLF

1S151 Winfield Road • Wheaton, IL 60189
630-668-5161 • www.cantigny.org
www.cantignygolf.com

Cantigny is the 500-acre former country estate of Robert R. McCormick (1880-1955), longtime editor and publisher of the *Chicago Tribune*. Located thirty-five miles west of Chicago, the park is owned and operated by the McCormick Foundation, a public charity. Attractions include the McCormick House (Colonel McCormick's mansion), First Division Museum, formal gardens, picnic grounds, and walking trails. The full-service Visitors Center features banquet and dining facilities, Bertie's Café, and the Cantigny Shop. Cantigny Golf is located adjacent to the park and offers twenty-seven championship holes plus the Cantigny Golf Academy and Cantigny Youth Links, a nine-hole course just for kids. Throughout the year, Cantigny is host to many special events and festivals, plus educational lectures, horticultural workshops, and concerts. The park is a popular venue for weddings and receptions as well. More information, including a calendar of upcoming events, is online at Cantigny.org.

McCormick House

Cantigny Rose Garden

Eggs in a Basket

2 slices bread, rye or your choice
Butter
2 eggs
Sharp Cheddar cheese, shredded
Salt and pepper to taste

Cut a hole in center of bread slices, being careful to avoid damaging the crust; hole should cover most of the bread. Add butter to a skillet over medium heat; place bread in skillet. Crack 1 egg in each bread basket; flip when eggs are cooked on 1 side (about 2 to 4 minutes). Sprinkle cheese over top of baskets; sprinkle with salt and pepper. Cover pan with lid to melt cheese. Plate and serve.

Four Lakes Alpine Snowsports

Four Lakes Alpine Snowsports

Mid-December to Mid-March

5750 Lakeside Drive • Lisle, IL 60532
630-964-2550 • www.fourlakessnowsports.com

Four Lakes has the "Anyone Can Do" attitude and wants to help you learn to ski or snowboard. The Snowsports School is ready to get you started and its instructors are always committed to teaching students to ski and snowboard safely and always in control so they are not only proficient, but most importantly, can have lots of fun. The floodlights turn night into day so you can enjoy your favorite sport even when the sun goes down. The award-winning terrain park has received accolades from skiers and snowboarders alike. Even when there's no snow in your backyard, they have plenty. So come on out and get on the snow. Four Lakes Alpine Snowsports builds passion for generations past, present, and future.

Breakfast Zucchini Pie

3 to 4 medium zucchini, grated
½ pound bacon
½ pound sausage
1 medium onion, diced
Salt and pepper to taste
1 cup grated sharp Cheddar cheese
3 eggs
¾ cup biscuit mix
1½ cups milk

Preheat oven to 400°. Grease a 9x13-inch baking pan; place zucchini in bottom. In a skillet, cook bacon; chop. Add bacon to top of zucchini. Cook sausage and onion in pan until browned; place over bacon. Add salt and pepper; top with cheese. Using a blender, blend eggs, biscuit mix and milk 15 seconds; pour over zucchini mixture. Bake 30 minutes; cool 5 minutes before eating.

Allyn House

Soups & Salads

Spicy Cheeseburger Soup

1½ cups water
2 cups peeled and cubed potatoes
2 small carrots, grated
1 small onion, chopped
4 teaspoons minced garlic
1 tablespoon beef bouillon granules
½ teaspoon salt
1 pound ground beef, cooked and drained
2½ cups milk, divided
3 tablespoons all-purpose flour
8 ounces American cheese, cubed
½ teaspoon cayenne pepper
½ pound bacon, cooked and crumbled

In a large saucepan over medium-high heat, combine water, potatoes, carrots, onion, garlic, bouillon and salt; bring to a boil. Reduce heat, cover; simmer 15 to 20 minutes or until potatoes are tender. Stir in beef and 2 cups milk; heat through. Combine flour with remaining milk until smooth; gradually stir into soup. Bring to boil; cook and stir 2 minutes till thickened. Reduce heat; stir in cheese until melted. Add cayenne pepper. Top with bacon before serving. Yields about 2 quarts.

Edinger's Filling Station
City of Pontiac

City of Pontiac

115 West Howard Street • Pontiac, IL 61764
800-835-2055 • 815-844-5847 • www.visitpontiac.org

Pontiac, Illinois, is one of the most popular destinations along historic Route 66. The quaint, turn-of-the-century shopping district features colorful murals, unique shops, and a collection of beautifully painted "Art Cars." Visitors will enjoy small town hospitality, unique walking tours, and fantastic food. The Illinois Route 66 Museum, the Pontiac-Oakland Automobile Museum, the Museum of the Gilding Arts, and the Livingston County War Museum are featured attractions in Pontiac. Summer fun includes street festivals, live entertainment, classic car shows, parades, and weekly farmer's markets. Music concerts and dinner theater at the Eagle Performing Arts Center and live drama in the park add to the year's excitement. Every visitor should remember to pick up a VIP button at the Route 66 Museum to receive special discounts from many of the local shops. Call or go online to receive a Pontiac visitor's packet.

Cabbage Soup

1 (1-pound) green cabbage
3 tablespoons butter
3 medium shallots, chopped
1 large russet potato, peeled and chopped
Salt and pepper to taste
Sour cream
Minced fresh parsley

Quarter cabbage, remove core and thinly slice crosswise. You should have about 5 to 6 cups cabbage. Using a Dutch oven, bring 3 quarts water to a boil; add cabbage. Cook 1 minute; drain. Melt butter in Dutch oven; add shallots and potato. Cook, stirring, 2 minutes. Add cabbage, salt, pepper and 5 cups water; bring to a boil. Cover; cook 20 minutes or until potato is tender. Ladle soup into bowls; add a dollop of sour cream to each bowl with parsley sprinkled over top. A final grinding of pepper over top is also nice. Makes 7 to 8 cups soup. Enjoy.

Illinois
Skydiving Center

1650 West Ottawa Road • Paxton, IL 60957
217-841-8881 • www.illinoisskydivingcenter.com

At Illinois Skydiving Center you'll get the personal attention you deserve. All instructors are expert skydivers and USPA certified. Their safety record, friendly atmosphere, and customer service reputation set them apart from every other skydiving center. During tandem jumps, students are strapped to a certified instructor who pulls the cord and directs the movements of the parachute as guests take in breathtaking views of the landscape, local tributaries, and central-state volcanoes before their feet land safely on the ground. Illinois Skydiving Center even offers helicopter jumps for those who are squeamish about jumping from an airplane.

Chowder

Olney is the county seat of Richland County. Richland County is famous for chowder!

1 bunch celery, sliced
2 pounds onions, sliced
2 sticks butter
1 head cabbage, cut into chunks or shredded
2 pounds dry lima beans, soaked overnight in water and drained
1 pound carrots, sliced into large pieces
8 to 10 pound turkey, cooked and deboned (save broth)

8 to 10-pound beef roast, cooked and deboned (save broth)
1 (1.9 ounce) box onion soup mix
10 pounds potatoes, peeled and cubed
1½ gallons green beans, drained
1½ gallons whole-kernel corn, drained
5 chicken bouillon cubes
5 beef bouillon cubes
1 gallon whole tomatoes
8 (8-ounce) cans tomato sauce

In a large stockpot, saute celery and onions in butter until tender; add cabbage, lima beans, carrots and meat broth. (If there is not enough liquid, add small amounts of water and bouillon to cover ingredients.) Sprinkle in soup mix; cook over medium heat until lima beans are beginning to soften. Add potatoes; cook 20 minutes. Add remaining ingredients. Simmer over low heat 1 hour (less if you test vegetables to be sure they aren't getting mushy). Season to taste. Yields: approximately 10 gallons.

City of Olney

City of Olney

300 South Whittle Avenue • Olney, IL 62450
618-395-7302 • www.ci.olney.il.us

If you are wanting to explore Illinois, we dare you to venture off the beaten path to explore a little town called Olney. Olney's biggest claim to fame is its population of albino white squirrels. These squirrels were first discovered in the area in the early 1900's and remain there today. The world is noticing, and featuring the town and its critters on various television programs. They have also been found by the off-beat blog called *Quirky Travel Guy* and PBS Digital Studios' *The Good Stuff*.

If rare, albino squirrels aren't your thing, you will find Olney's quaint community and slower pace quite refreshing. Olney is home to various local eateries, each with their signature dishes. Additionally, Olney is host to three beautiful lakes that are known to fishermen all over the state for their beauty, landscape, and of course.... great fishing!

Shop, dine, play...Olney has it all!

BLT Chopped Salad with Avocado

Lime Vinaigrette:

2 tablespoons olive oil
2 tablespoons apple cider vinegar
½ lime, juiced
⅛ teaspoon salt
⅛ teaspoon pepper
½ teaspoon sugar

Salad:

3 cups chopped butter lettuce
1 cup chopped fresh arugula
1 cup diced tomatoes
¾ cup sweet corn, canned or freshly grilled
1 ripe avocado, chopped
4 slices bacon, cooked and crumbled
¼ cup feta cheese, crumbled

In a small bowl, whisk together olive oil, vinegar, lime juice, salt, pepper and sugar to make a vinaigrette; set aside. (If you want to make vinaigrette ahead of time, it will keep in refrigerator several days.) When ready to serve, combine lettuce, arugula, tomatoes, corn and avocado in a large bowl. Fold in bacon and feta cheese. Top with vinaigrette and serve immediately. Serves 2 to 4. Enjoy!

Prairie View Garden Center & Farm Market

Apple Chicken Salad

½ cup fat-free yogurt
¼ cup orange juice
½ cup Kuipers apple jelly, melted
1 tablespoon lemon juice
¼ teaspoon salt, optional
3 cups diced cooked chicken
2 cups finely sliced celery
3 fresh-picked Kuipers apples, diced with skin on
½ cup chopped peanuts

In a large bowl, mix yogurt, orange juice, jelly and lemon juice; add chicken, celery and apples. Toss gently to coat all pieces. Season with salt; chill until ready to serve. Sprinkle with peanuts; serve. 8 servings.

Kuipers Family Farm

Grilled Caesar Salad

¼ red onion
¼ fresh red bell pepper
1 tablespoon olive oil, plus more for coating lettuce
¼ cup quality balsamic vinegar
½ head romaine lettuce
Salt and pepper to taste
2 tablespoons Caesar dressing
3 tablespoons shaved Parmesan cheese

Chop onion and bell pepper into bite-size pieces. Coat with 1 tablespoon olive oil and drizzle with balsamic vinegar. Set aside 15 minutes while completing recipe. Coat romaine with olive oil, salt and pepper. Grill over medium heat 4 minutes each side. Remove core and plate grilled romaine; top with dressing and cheese. Pour reserved vegetables over top including the balsamic. Top with fresh ground pepper. Serve and enjoy!

Jeff Shapiro, Real Urban Barbecue
Little Bear Rib Fest

Waldorf Salad

This makes a great summer salad, and can also be served with smoked chicken breast.

1½ cups red seedless grapes, sliced lengthwise
1½ cups green seedless grapes, sliced lengthwise
1½ cups black seedless grapes, sliced lengthwise
5 medium stalks celery, chopped
4 medium sweet red apples, cored, chopped and rinsed in lemon juice
4 medium Granny Smith apples, cored, chopped and rinsed in lemon juice
1 cup dried cranberries
1 tablespoon cinnamon
1 to 2 cups vanilla yogurt, enough to lightly cover or to taste
4 tablespoons butter
3 cups brown sugar
¼ cup water
2 tablespoons pumpkin pie spice
4 cups walnuts
1 teaspoon coarse salt
1 large package mixed organic spring greens
Poppy seed dressing

Mix grapes, celery, apples, cranberries, cinnamon and yogurt in a large bowl. Cover and refrigerate while preparing remaining recipe. For praline walnuts, melt butter in a saucepan over medium-high heat; add brown sugar, water and pumpkin pie spice. Mix in walnuts and salt. Cook, constantly stirring, until boiling. Lower heat to medium-low and reduce until caramelized. Immediately pour onto greased cookie sheet; it will harden as it cools. Chop before serving. To serve Waldorf Salad, place a bed of mixed greens in bottom of salad dish. Top with 3 cups fruit mix. Sprinkle with praline walnuts and drizzle poppy seed dressing on top. Serve.

Terri Smith, 718 Brew Café

Greater Metropolis Tourism

1308 East 5th Street • Metropolis, IL 62960
618-524-5025 • www.metropolistourism.com

Metropolis is where heroes and history meet on the shores of the majestic Ohio River. This All-American town has been a must-visit destination for Superman fans since being declared the adopted "Home of Superman" by National Periodical Publications (D.C. Comics) in 1972. In the previous forty-five years, Metropolis has become more than a comic mecca. With world-renown events that celebrate the history, hunting, and yes, even Superman, as well as an action-packed casino and outdoor wonders that take you through the Shawnee National Forest or even under water through a Boeing 727 Airplane, Metropolis is a town that has been added to many bucket lists.

Monday–Friday: 9:00 am to 4:00 pm

Kale Salad

The best kale to use for this recipe is lacinato kale, also known as Tuscan, dinosaur or black kale. It has a beautiful dark green exterior and the ribs are not as large or woody as curly kale.

4 pounds kale, ribs removed
1 cup rice wine vinegar
4 teaspoons sugar
2 teaspoons kosher salt
½ teaspoon pepper
3 cloves garlic, crushed
3 small shallots, chopped
2 teaspoon Dijon mustard (or grainy mustard)
2 teaspoons fresh lemon juice
2 cups olive oil

Lay kale flat and layer leaves on top of one another. Thinly slice kale into small ribbons, ½- to ¾-inch wide. Set aside (can be prepared up to 2 days in advance). Make lemon-mustard vinaigrette by combining vinegar, sugar, salt, pepper, garlic, shallots, Dijon and lemon juice in a blender; purée. While blender is running, pour olive oil through top in a long, thin stream. This will allow the oil to emulsify. You should have about 3½ cups dressing. This will keep up to 2 weeks in the refrigerator. Before using, allow it to come to room temperature and stir or shake well. This salad is a blank slate. You can add whatever you would like to it and it will taste great.

Note: Great spring variation is to add quartered strawberries, toasted whole almonds, chopped rendered bacon and Parmesan cheese. Later summer variation is to add small beets (wrap in foil with salt and olive oil and roast at 375°) cut into quarters, toasted chopped pecans and herbed goat cheese.

Molly's Kitchen and Bar

Molly's Kitchen and Bar

110 West Market Street • Mount Carroll, IL 61053
815-906-0052 • www.mollysmountcarroll.com • Find us on Facebook

Molly's Kitchen and Bar serves classic cuisine and cocktails made from scratch. Chef Molly McDonough uses the freshest ingredients possible, many locally sourced, to achieve the flavors and presentations that make dining at Molly's a satisfying experience. The bar program uses freshly squeezed juices and high-quality spirits to make delicious cocktails that complement the food. Focusing on a small menu allows them to ensure that great care is taken with every dish. Relax in small-town comfort in the historic, restored 1865 building, featuring two suites, combining rural charm with contemporary amenities and style. Guests will find fresh fruit, yogurt, coffee, and tea, as well as fruit juice in the kitchen. Both suites are decorated with the work of local artists, as well as period industrial light fixtures. Spend the day exploring the historic buildings and architecture of Mount Carroll, antiques, and the beautiful pastoral landscape of the Driftless Area. Then, come home to cocktails and a delicious meal downstairs at Molly's.

Wednesday–Saturday: 4:30 pm to 9:00 pm
Sunday: 10:00 am to 2:00 pm

Broccoli Salad

1 medium bunch raw broccoli, finely chopped with stems and buds
½ pound bacon, cooked crisp and crumbled
2 cups halved seedless grapes
1 cup diced celery
4 to 5 green onions, chopped
1 (4-ounce) package slivered almonds
1 cup mayonnaise
½ cup sugar
1 tablespoon vinegar

In a large bowl, add broccoli, bacon, grapes, celery, green onions and almonds; stir to mix. In a smaller bowl, combine mayonnaise, sugar and vinegar; mix well. Refrigerate at least 1 hour. Just before serving, add dressing and toss well to mix. This is a delicious recipe and perfect for any occasion.

Esther Goebbert
Goebbert's Farm & Garden Center

Goebbert's Farm & Garden Center

Mid-April through October 31st

40 West Higgins Road • South Barrington, IL 60010
847-428-6727 • www.pumpkinfarms.com • www.facebook.com/goebbertsfarm

Goebbert's Farm, a local and family-owned business since 1948, is a three season farm with many offerings from mid-April to the end of October. In the spring, we are a garden center and nursery with a large variety of plants and gardening materials. At the beginning of July, we offer homegrown vegetables and fruits as a fresh produce stand. In late September, we begin our Fall Festival with activities and fun for the whole family to enjoy. Throughout our three seasons, we offer a family-owned and operated business that truly loves being your local source for plants, food, and fun. We encourage all our guests to check us out during each season to begin harvesting family memories at Goebbert's.

Daily: 9:00 am to 6:00 pm

Sweet Apple Coleslaw

A favorite in our dining room.

5 cups shredded cabbage
2 stalks celery, finely chopped
2 Red Delicious apples, cored and finely chopped
½ cup raisins
1 cup nonfat mayonnaise
½ cup nonfat sour cream
½ cup sugar
¼ cup apple cider vinegar

In a large bowl, combine cabbage, celery, apples and raisins. In another bowl, mix mayonnaise, sour cream, sugar and vinegar; toss with cabbage mixture. Use as much dressing as you want. Serves 8 to 10. If coleslaw is too tart, add ½ teaspoon salt.

Royal Oak Farm

Visit McHenry County
Royal Oak Farm Apple Orchard

August–November

15908 Hebron Road • Harvard, IL 60033
815-648-4141 • www.royaloakfarmorchard.com • Find us on Facebook

Four generations of Royal Oak Farm family live and work at the orchard, with backgrounds ranging from builders and musicians to booksellers and athletes. Each has brought his or her gifts and talents to work at the orchard. When visiting the orchard, don't miss Amaze 'N Apples, the country's first and only apple tree maze! Wander its one and a half miles of walking trails while picking from nine different varieties of apple trees. When you find your way out, stop by the bakery for fresh apple cider donuts or discover beautiful fall decor for your home. Make sure to visit the Country Kitchen Restaurant to sample their famous caramelized apple cinnamon French toast for breakfast or their renowned chicken pot pie for lunch.

Banana Salad

2 eggs, well beaten
¾ cup milk
1 tablespoon vinegar
¼ cup butter
2 cups sugar
3 tablespoons flour
Pinch salt
5 to 6 bananas
¾ cup chopped peanuts

In a double boiler over medium-high heat, cook eggs, milk, vinegar, butter, sugar, flour and salt; stir constantly until mixture begins to thicken. Remove from heat; cool completely. In a bowl, slice bananas; pour cooked mixture over bananas. Add peanuts. Ready to serve.

Hornbaker Gardens

The Barn at Hornbaker Gardens

Hornbaker Gardens

22937 1140 North Avenue • Princeton, IL 61356
815-659-3282 • www.hornbakergardens.com

Experience Hornbaker Gardens: a destination garden center, arboretum, and botanical gardens in one location. Stroll through the extensive display gardens featuring mature plantings of hostas and other perennials in both sun and shade environments, a collection of unusual trees and shrubs, water features, and garden art. The garden center stocks over 400 varieties of hostas along with a large selection of daylilies, trees and shrubs, grasses, and much more. You'll also find bronze, granite, and metal garden art, pottery, and unique items in our gift shop. The Barn, opened in 2015, is an event center hosting weddings and special events. Be sure to stop by historic Princeton while in the area to pick up some local art, tasty treats, and explore unique shopping. For thirty years the Hornbaker family has been welcoming gardening enthusiasts from all over the Midwest and they hope to see you soon.

Raspberry Salad

2 (3-ounce) packages raspberry Jell-O
2 cups boiling water
1 pint vanilla ice cream
1 (6-ounce) can frozen lemonade
1 (10-ounce) bag frozen red raspberries
1 banana, sliced

Set raspberries and lemonade out to thaw slightly. In a bowl, dissolve Jell-O in boiling water. Add ice cream by spoonful and stir until melted. Stir in raspberries, lemonade and banana slices. Chill until set.

Long Hollow Canopy Tours

Mandarin Delight Fruit Salad

1 (1.34-ounce) box cook & serve sugar-free vanilla pudding
1 (3-ounce) box tapioca pudding
1 (.32-ounce) box orange sugar-free gelatin
½ cup sugar
3 cups water
1 (16-ounce) container Cool Whip
2 (29-ounce) cans Mandarin oranges, well drained

In a saucepan, blend together puddings, gelatin, sugar and water; cook over medium heat until mixture thickens. Set aside to cool. Fold in Cool Whip and oranges; refrigerate until ready to serve. Everyone will love it!

Allyn House

Vegetables & Side Dishes

Ruth's Sweet Potato Casserole

Makes 4 Servings

INGREDIENTS

Crust Mixture:
¾ cup brown sugar
¼ cup flour
¾ cup chopped nuts
  (pecans preferred)
¼ cup melted butter

Sweet Potato Mixture:
¾ cup sugar
¼ teaspoon salt
½ teaspoon vanilla
2 cups mashed sweet
  potatoes

1 egg, well beaten
¼ cup butter

PROCESS

1. Combine Crust Mixture in mixing bowl and put to one side.

2. Combine Sweet Potato Mixture ingredients in a mixing bowl in the order listed.
   Combine thoroughly.

3. Pour Sweet Potato Mixture into buttered baking dish.

4. Sprinkle Crust Mixture evenly onto surface of Sweet Potato Mixture.

5. Bake for 30 minutes at 350°. Allow to set for at least 30 minutes before serving.

Ruth's Chris
Barrington Brew Fest

Barrington Brew Fest

2nd Saturday in July

Downtown Barrington • Barrington, IL 60010
847-381-5030 • www.barringtonbrewfest.com

With nearly fifty brewers showcasing more than ninety different brews, Barrington's Brew Fest has become the foremost beer fest in the Northwest suburbs. Set in downtown Barrington, in the center of town by the Metra tracks, the Barrington Brew Fest is held the second Saturday every July and benefits the Barrington Area Council on Aging. BACOA is a vital resource for aging adults, care partners, and families as they navigate the challenges of aging. From respite care to general information and support, BACOA is the organization residents turn to when trying to understand issues surrounding aging.

3:00 pm to 7:00 pm

Hash Brown Casserole

This recipe pairs well with Illinois Vignoles wine!

1 (24-ounce) package refrigerated or frozen hash browns
1 cup shredded Cheddar cheese
1 (10.75-ounce) can cream of potato soup
½ cup milk
½ cup sliced green onion
1 tablespoon butter, melted
1 teaspoon finely chopped garlic
⅓ cup grated Parmesan cheese
Paprika

Heat oven to 350°. Spray a 2-quart casserole with nonstick cooking spray. In a large bowl, combine all ingredients except Parmesan cheese and paprika; stir to mix well. Spread in baking dish. Sprinkle with Parmesan cheese and paprika. Bake, uncovered, 55 to 60 minutes or until potatoes are tender and center is heated through.

Illinois Grape Growers & Vintners Association

Illinois Grape Growers & Vintners Association

2900 Greenbriar Drive • Springfield, IL 62704
217-726-8518 • www.illinoiswine.com

ILLINOISWINE
www.illinoiswine.com

Winter Wine Festival - 4th Friday in February

Ottawa 2 Rivers Wine Festival - 2nd weekend in June

Illinois State Fair Wine Experience
during the Illinois State Fair in August

Vintage Illinois Wine Festival - 3rd weekend in September

Great River Grape Escape - 4th weekend in September

With more than 100 wineries, over 450 vineyards, 1100 grape-producing acres, and at least 100 miles of wine trails, it's no wonder Illinois is Wine! Illinois offers award-winning vintages and an impressive range of grape varietals. There are no vintners friendlier and no vineyards or trails more scenic, with endless rivers and valleys crossing the state. Illinois winemakers work with French-American hybrid grapes, as well as vinifera and native varieties to blend and produce a diverse range of high-quality wines. From sweet, refreshing whites to dry, robust reds, Illinois offers every palate a favorite flavor and plenty to try. The Illinois Grape Growers & Vintners Association invites you to join in all the fun Illinois wine has to offer. Because Illinois is Wine!

Cheesy Mashed Potatoes

½ pound potatoes, peeled and chunked
1½ tablespoons butter
¼ cup whipping cream
1 teaspoon minced garlic
4 ounces Marcoot Jersey Creamery Tomme, sliced in small strips
Salt and pepper to taste

In a saucepan over medium-high heat, boil potatoes in salted water to cover until tender; drain. In a small saucepan, while potatoes are cooking, warm butter, cream and garlic until almost simmering. Put potatoes in a Dutch oven over low heat; mash half the potatoes. Stir in cream mixture; mash again. Gradually stir in Tomme; add salt and pepper. Continue to stir until potatoes are desired consistency.

Marcoot Jersey Creamery

Marcoot Jersey Creamery

526 Dudleyville Road • Greenville, IL 62246
618-664-1110 • www.marcootjerseycreamery.com

Marcoot Jersey Creamery is a seventh-generation, family-owned Jersey dairy farm in Greenville, where only the highest-quality artisan and farmstead cheeses are handcrafted. You will enjoy watching the cheese making process through large viewing windows in the creamery and the "field-to-fork" video about the family farm. You may purchase farmstead and artisan cheeses, plus custard-style ice cream at the country store. Tours of the facilities are available; visit the website for details. The Marcoot family says, "We are excited to bring our family's passion and tradition to your table!"

Country Store Hours
April 1st to October 31st
Monday–Friday: 10:00 am to 5:00 pm
Saturday: 10:00 am to 3:00 pm

November 1st to March 31st
Monday–Friday: 10:00 am to 4:00 pm
Saturday: 10:00 am to 3:00 pm

Kroppkakor

10 to 12 medium potatoes, peeled and boiled
1 egg
1¼ cups all-purpose flour
1 onion, finely chopped
8 ounces salt pork, cut into small pieces
4 tablespoons butter
1 teaspoon cracked allspice
Salt

Mash potatoes. Stir in egg and flour, making a smooth dough. Fry onion and salt pork in butter until onions are soft. Add allspice and salt to taste. Simmer salted water in a large uncovered pot. Shape dough into a log and cut in 3 equal pieces. Cut each in half then half again to make 12 pieces. Make a little pocket in each and fill with about 1 tablespoon filling; close and shape into a ball. Put about 4 to 5 at a time in simmering water and cook 5 to 6 minutes. Kroppkakor will sink then float to top when ready. Dumplings can also be cut in half and fried in butter. Serve with melted butter and lingonberries.

Stockholm Inn

Stockholm Inn

2420 Charles Street • Rockford, IL 61108
815-397-3534 • www.StockholmInn.com

The spirit of hospitality is the hallmark of Stockholm Inn, where they go far beyond inviting soon-to-be friends to the table. Stockholm Inn welcomes you and your guests with charming surroundings and friendly greetings. From their world-famous Swedish pancakes to a wide variety of handcrafted dishes made from the freshest ingredients, they offer a unique dining experience in a truly distinct atmosphere. Enjoy live music on Friday nights, the Swedish Smorgasbord on Saturday evenings, and the breakfast brunch on Saturday and Sunday mornings.

Monday–Thursday: 7:00 am to 7:00 pm
Friday & Saturday: 7:00 am to 2:00 pm
Sunday: 7:00 am to 2:00 pm

Stockholm Inn
® SWEDISH TRADITIONS. SWEDISH HERITAGE.

Voted Best Breakfast & Brunch

Escalloped Corn

1 stick butter (or oleo), melted
1 (15-ounce) can whole-kernel corn
1 (15-ounce) can cream-style corn
2 eggs, well beaten
1 cup sour cream
1 (8-ounce) package corn muffin mix

Preheat oven to 350°. In a large bowl, combine all ingredients. Pour into baking dish. Bake until golden brown.

Ruth Ann Metzen
Rock Falls

Rock Falls

603 West 10th Street • Rock Falls, IL 61071
815-622-1106 • www.visitrockfalls.com

Welcome to Rock Falls. Conveniently located right off interstate 88, they have attractions, events, and lodging waiting for you and your family. Take time off, take a deep breath, and enjoy northwest Illinois. You will find your home away from home while visiting this neck of the woods. With two communities hugging the banks of the Rock River, they have a blend of unique histories, the stunning Rock River, Hennepin Feeder Canal, and gorgeous countrysides. The area boasts outdoor fun and fitness and the diverse cultural backgrounds create a melting pot of unparalleled festivals and events.

French-Fried Mushrooms

1 pound mushrooms
1 egg
¼ cup milk
½ cup flour
½ teaspoon baking powder
¼ teaspoon salt
1 tablespoon shortening

Remove caps from mushrooms; set aside. In a bowl. Combine egg, milk, flour, baking powder, salt and shortening. Dip caps in batter; fry in deep-fat fryer at 375° until lightly browned. Serve hot. Cauliflower florets can be made the same way.

International Annual Houby Fest

International Annual Houby Fest

October

Central Avenue and Lombard on Cermak Road • Cicero, IL 60804
708-656-3600 • www.thetownofcicero.com

The Houby Parade is the highlight of a week-long festival on Cermak Road celebrated each year by the Town of Cicero and the City of Berwyn. Held on a Sunday afternoon in early October, the parade honors the humble mushroom—"houby" in Czech—and recalls the eastern European origins of many residents of the two communities during the twentieth century. Marching down the principal commercial street, which unites the people of Berwyn and Cicero, are units representing their business, civic, ethnic, and religious lives. They are led by their elected officials and large contingents of police and fire personnel, as well as veterans of the armed forces. This popular tradition began in 1968 under the sponsorship of the Cermak Road Business Association and will be celebrating fifty years in 2018. It has been maintained in recent years by a committee of prominent citizens from both municipalities.

Coconut Carrots

2 cups grated carrots
1 cup grated fresh coconut
¾ cup brown sugar
½ cup water

Preheat oven to 350°. In a bowl, mix carrots, coconut and sugar. Place in a buttered baking dish; pour water over top. Bake 30 minutes.

Kayak Chicago

1220 West LeMoyne Avenue • Chicago, IL 60642
312-852-9258 • www.kayakchicago.com
Four locations, check the website for details:
Chicago River • Montrose Beach • North Avenue Beach • UIC Pool

Started in 1999, Kayak Chicago is Chicago's premier, full-service watersports outfitter, offering the highest-quality instruction and trips with fully certified instructors and guides. Founder and owner Dave Olson began Kayak Chicago, teaching classes to people of all abilities from athletes to people with physical disabilities who could enjoy kayaking as a form of rehabilitation. Today, Kayak Chicago offers guided tours, classes, and rentals at four locations situated throughout Chicago. If you're in the mood for a leisurely paddle along the river, or ready to enjoy a gorgeous view of the city skyline, you can safely kayak at the Chicago River or two beach locations. Beginner classes are also available at the UIC Natatorium. Kayak Chicago loves kayaking and wants to share the fun, knowledge, and on-water experience with you. Come learn the skills and techniques you need to explore life from the water.

Monday–Sunday: 10:00 am to 7:00 pm

Spinach

6 slices bacon
1½ pounds baby spinach leaves, washed and drained
2 teaspoons salt
¾ teaspoon black pepper
1 tablespoon butter
Lemon

Cook bacon in a large covered skillet; remove to drain on a paper towel, saving 2 tablespoons grease in pan. Add spinach, salt and pepper; cover skillet. Cook 2 minutes on medium-high heat. Remove cover and cook on high, stirring with a wooden spoon, until spinach is wilted. Using a slotted spoon, lift spinach to a serving bowl; top with butter and a good squeeze of lemon. Serve hot.

Annual
Popeye Festival

1st Weekend after Labor Day

Chester, IL 62233

618-826-5114 • www.popeyepicnic.com • www.chesterill.com

Popeye the Sailor Man, a six-foot tall 900-pound bronze statue, has been overlooking the Mississippi River in Segar Park, next to the Chester Bridge, since the summer of 1977. And for more than thirty years the City of Chester has hosted the Annual Popeye Picnic which is always held the first weekend after Labor Day. Thousands of people come from all over to enjoy a weekend full of activities including a carnival with rides, games, good food, local talent, and a huge parade honoring our most beloved Sailor Man.

Chester, Illinois, home of Popeye the Sailor Man

Baked Brussels Sprouts with Bacon

20 Brussels sprouts
1 pound bacon, chopped
Olive oil
Salt and pepper to taste
Minced garlic to taste

Preheat oven to 400°. Cut Brussels sprouts in half, discarding the outer skin. Lay sprouts cut side up in a 9x13-inch baking dish. Cover sprouts with bacon, drizzle with olive oil and season with salt, pepper and garlic. Bake 20 minutes; stir. Continue to bake until bacon is crisp and Brussels sprouts begin to brown.

Four Lakes Snowsports

Acorn Squash Stuffed with Apples

3 acorn squash, cut in half lengthwise with seeds removed
5 tablespoons softened butter, divided
3 tart apples, peeled, cored and cut into chunks
¼ teaspoon salt
6 tablespoons golden raisins
6 tablespoons chopped walnuts
3 tablespoons brown sugar
1 teaspoon cinnamon
1 teaspoon nutmeg

Preheat oven to 375°. Cut a very thin slice off bottom to level squash to sit upright; place on baking sheet. Put ½ tablespoon butter in each squash half; cover with foil. Bake 25 minutes. In a mixing bowl, combine apples, salt, 2 tablespoons butter, golden raisins, walnuts, brown sugar, cinnamon and nutmeg; mix well. Spoon apple mixture into squash cavities, dividing it evenly between the 6 halves. Cover with foil; continue baking 20 minutes or until squash is tender.

Tanners Orchard

Pecan Squash Bake

This has been a Royal Oak Farm Restaurant favorite for years. Everyone wants this recipe, and it is also our family's Thanksgiving menu favorite.

2 cups butternut squash
⅓ cup plus 2 tablespoons butter, divided
¾ cup sugar
2 eggs, beaten
1 (5-ounce) can evaporated milk
1 teaspoon vanilla
½ cup Rice Krispies
¼ cup brown sugar
¼ cup chopped pecans

Preheat oven to 350°. Cook squash in pan of water on stove; drain and mash. Cream ⅓ cup butter and sugar in a bowl; beat in eggs, milk and vanilla. Stir in squash. Pour mixture into a greased 7x11-inch pan. Bake 45 minutes or until set. Melt remaining butter; mix with Rice Krispies, brown sugar and pecans. Pour over top.

Royal Oak Farm

Herbed Spaghetti Squash

1 medium spaghetti squash (about 3 pounds)
1 tablespoon olive oil
½ teaspoon dried basil
½ teaspoon dried oregano
½ teaspoon garlic powder
¼ teaspoon salt
¼ teaspoon black pepper

Preheat oven to 375°. Wash outside of squash; pat dry. Carefully cut squash in half from top to bottom. Scoop out seeds and stringy part with a large spoon; discard. Place squashhalves, cut side down, in a baking dish; add water to cover bottom of dish. Bake 45 to 60 minutes or until tender. Rake flesh of cooked squash with a fork into strands; add to a medium-sized bowl. Toss cooked squash with olive oil, herbs and spices. Serve hot.

D'Arcy's Pint

661 West Stanford Avenue • Springfield, IL 62704
217-492-8800 • www.darcyspintonline.com

D'Arcy's Pint is a simple bar with Irish and American pub fare, including horseshoe sandwiches, and a beer garden. Irish hospitality reigns supreme at D'Arcy's. Hallie Pierceall and Glenn Merriman opened D'Arcy's with the intention to make people feel comfortable enough to stay a while, just like a corner pub in Ireland. Weather permitting, you may want to socialize in the outdoor beer garden. Your experience won't be complete without trying their famous horseshoes, a unique regional specialty made of your choice of meat served over Texas toast, piled high with fries and topped with homemade cheese sauce. Enjoy the history of Springfield before coming in D'Arcy's for a great meal and pleasant conversation in a relaxing atmosphere. Capture your own bit o' Irish luck.

Monday–Saturday: 11:00 am to 1:00 pm
Sunday: Noon to 6:00 pm

Easy Apple and Squash Casserole

2½ cups raw, fresh-picked acorn or butternut squash from Kuipers, cut in 1-inch chunks
1½ cups fresh-picked Kuipers apples, peeled and cut in thick slices
¼ cup melted butter, divided
¼ cup brown sugar
1 teaspoon cinnamon
½ cup chopped pecans
Dash salt

Preheat oven to 350°. Using a 2-quart casserole dish, layer half the squash with half the apple slices; drizzle half the butter on top. In a saucepan, combine remaining butter, brown sugar, cinnamon, nuts and salt. Arrange remaining squash and apples in dish; pour butter-sugar mixture over them. Cover dish; bake 45 to 60 minutes until tender.

Kuipers Family Farm

Kuipers Family Farm

Open Daily Mid-August to December

1N318 Watson Road • Maple Park, IL 60151
815-827-5200 • www.kuipersfamilyfarm.com
www.facebook.com/kuipersfamilyfarm

This orchard and farm, situated on 230 acres of rolling Illinois farmland, is located just west of suburban Chicago and is open daily beginning in mid-August. Apple picking is weekends only, but freshly harvested apples can be purchased daily in the Orchard Shop where the aroma of fresh apple cider doughnuts, home-baked pies, fudge, pasteurized apple cider, and hand-spun caramel apples from The Orchard Bakery lingers in the air. The Orchard Shop is full of unique, farm-fresh, specialty foods and gift items for you to browse. Mid-September, the west side of the farm opens for some down-on-the-farm fun like The Maize Corn Maze, hayrides, farm animals, a haunted forest, tractor tire mountain, peddle tractor derby, nature walk, jumping pillows, pumpkin picking, and much more. November and December at the farm are dedicated to the holidays with pies and specialty foods for entertaining, unique gifts for giving, and of course, Christmas trees.

Heirloom Delicata Squash

This is for those who want a quick, gourmet appetizer, side or salad topping. Foxtrot Organic Farmer Ellen says: "It's so tender that we encourage you to eat the skin!"

1 Delicata squash
Grapeseed oil (or coconut oil) to taste
Steak seasoning to taste

Preheat oven to 425°. Slice squash down middle and scoop out seeds; slice into little arches. Toss squash with grapeseed oil and steak seasoning to taste. Bake 20 minutes or until both sides are caramelized; flip at 10 minutes.

Primrose Farm

Primrose Farm

Grounds Open Dawn to Dusk

5N726 Crane Road • St. Charles, IL 60175
630-513-4370 • www.primrosefarmpark.com

Experience farm life while you explore restored farm buildings, visit with farm animals and agricultural interpreters, stroll through more than 100 acres of historic and modern rural landscapes, or climb up on a vintage tractor in the fruit orchard. Exciting and educational activities await you in the farmyard

where you can hand-milk a Jersey cow. The opportunities to learn and play are endless. Drop-in programs are offered Wednesdays and Saturdays. Custom programs and birthday party packages are available, too. Admission is free.

Office Hours
Monday–Saturday: 8:00 am to 3:00 pm

Baked Sicilian Eggplant Parmesan

2 Sicilian eggplants
5 eggs
2 tablespoons milk
Salt and pepper to taste
2 cups Italian breadcrumbs
2 cups shredded Parmesan cheese
1 tablespoon oregano
1 tablespoon chopped fresh thyme
Mozzarella cheese, thin slices

Preheat oven to 350°. Wash eggplant and slice into ½-inch-thick rounds; set aside. In a bowl, whisk together eggs and milk seasoned with salt and pepper. In another bowl, combine breadcrumbs, Parmesan cheese, oregano and thyme. Dip each eggplant slice in milk mixture; shake off excess. Then dip into breadcrumb mixture, making sure to coat both sides. Arrange coated slices in a single layer on a baking sheet that has been sprayed with a light coat of olive oil or cooking oil spray. Bake 20 to 25 minutes. Turn oven to broil; top each eggplant slice with a mozzarella slice. Broil until mozzarella is golden brown and bubbly. Enjoy!

Prairie View Garden Center & Farm Market

Prairie View Garden Center & Farm Market

Mid-April–October

48W130 IL Route 72 • Hampshire, IL 60140
847-683-4970 • www.prairieviewfarmmarket.com

Prairie View is located where small towns and acres of farm fields begin for a relaxing and beautiful stop along your journey. Opening in April, Prairie View will blow your mind with the explosion of color that surrounds you in their greenhouses. Every hanging basket and container garden is designed, planted, and cared for by Prairie

View's friendly staff. Once summer arrives, the harvest begins and their market becomes a wonderland of things to tantalize your taste buds. Fresh pies and cookies are baked on-site in Prairie View's own kitchen. The bounty of their daily harvest fills the market. Mounds of colorful fruits and vegetables—fresh from the field—are waiting to find a spot on your dinner table. Fall brings you back to the days when you stopped along the roadside to pick out the perfect pumpkin and get a sweet treat. The ever-changing Prairie View makes stopping there a delight throughout their season.

Monday–Friday: 9:00 am to 6:00 pm
Saturday & Sunday: 9:00 am to 5:00 pm

Asparagus and Crisp Prosciutto Wraps

1 tablespoon extra-virgin olive oil
16 slices prosciutto
16 fresh asparagus spears, trimmed

Preheat oven to 450°. Line baking sheet with aluminum foil; coat with olive oil. Wrap 1 slice prosciutto around each asparagus, starting at bottom and spiraling to top; place on pan. Bake 5 minutes; remove from heat. Shake pan to roll spears over; cook another 5 minutes. When asparagus is tender and prosciutto is crisp, serve immediately.

Jasper County
Chamber of Commerce

124 South Van Buren • Newton, IL 62448
618-783-3399 • www.jasperchamber.com • Find us on Facebook

Jasper County is a wonderful place to enjoy the great outdoors with lots of places to fish, hunt, canoe, and go birding. Jasper County is the home of the late Burl Ives, who is most famously known as Sam the Snowman in *Rudolph the Red-Nosed Reindeer*. The Jasper County Chamber of Commerce hosts two large festivals a year. FarmFest is the weekend after Memorial Day, and Fall Festival is the weekend after Labor Day. Both festivals are full of family-oriented fun, food, games, and crafts.

Hidden Vegetable Pasta Sauce

2 medium carrots
1 small zucchini
1 cup broccoli florets
1 small onion
10 fresh button mushrooms
3 tablespoons olive oil
2 teaspoons minced garlic
4 (8-ounce) cans no-salt-
   added tomato sauce

2 (6-ounce) cans tomato paste
½ teaspoon dried oregano
½ teaspoon dried basil
½ teaspoon dried thyme
½ teaspoon dried parsley
½ teaspoon salt
½ teaspoon black pepper
2 pounds cooked pasta

Using a food processor, mince all vegetables. Heat oil over medium heat in a 6-quart Dutch oven. Add garlic and minced vegetables; cook, stirring frequently, 5 minutes. Add all other ingredients except pasta and mix well. Partially cover pot and bring to a boil over high heat. Reduce heat to low, partially cover pot, and simmer 45 minutes, stirring occasionally. Serve with prepared pasta.

Keller's Farmstand

Keller's Farmstand

Oswego • Naperville • Plainfield

www.KellersFarmstand.com

The Kellers, a five-generation farming family, have been in the Naperville area since 1852 and, like any other growing business, expanded to two more locations: Oswego and Plainfield. Springtime brings a variety of gorgeous, homegrown, premium flowers, hanging baskets, mixed planters, and specialty annuals as well as local perennials. Keller's offers a large selection of hard-to-find vegetable plants as well as your favorite herbs. They grow over fourty acres of sweet corn every summer, so you can enjoy mouth-watering corn from mid-July until October. Homegrown vegetables are picked and delivered to all Keller's locations daily. Also provided are other Illinois-grown favorites, such as peaches, watermelons, and muskmelons. The Oswego farm offers daily seasonal apple picking and pumpkin picking. In the fall, the Oswego location features special Saturday- and Sunday-only festivities, including a ten-acre corn maze, wagon rides, animal barn, kids' play area, and concession stands. Don't leave without trying the delicious apple cider donuts!

Fettuccini Alfredo

1 (9-ounce) package fresh fettuccini
¾ cup heavy cream
3 tablespoons butter
¼ teaspoon nutmeg
½ to ¾ cup grated Parmesan cheese
⅛ teaspoon fresh ground pepper

In a large pot of boiling salted water, cook pasta until barely tender; drain. In a large skillet over medium-low heat, combine cream, butter, nutmeg and noodles. Cook, tossing gently, until sauce reduces to a slightly thickened creamy consistency, usually 3 to 5 minutes. Add cheese and pepper; toss again. Serve immediately.

The Spirit of Peoria Riverboat

100 Water Street • Peoria, IL 61602
309-637-8000 • www.spiritofpeoria.com

Ever want to float down the river and pretend you are Huckleberry Finn? Well Captain Alex Grieves will give you the chance to make your dream come true. Come join a cruise up and down the Illinois and Mississippi Rivers. You may take a day cruise or enjoy up to a 5-day, 4-night cruise aboard this big paddleboat marvel. The Spirit of Peoria is one of a few paddleboats still navigating the nation's rivers. Spend relaxing days enjoying the river scenery, eating buffet meals, live entertainment, storytelling, and wildlife sightings. Passengers may even get to see Mark Twain. Life on the river is an ever-changing fascination with nature. Enjoy the slower pace of life on this unique paddleboat!

Vermicelli Pasta

1 (16-ounce) package vermicelli noodles, broken up
⅓ cup lemon juice
⅓ cup oil
1½ tablespoons Accent seasoning
2 tablespoons seasoning salt
¾ cup chopped celery
¾ cup chopped onion
¾ cup chopped red or green bell pepper
2 (4-ounce) cans sliced black olives, drained
1 cup mayonnaise

In a stockpot of boiling water, cook noodles 6 minutes; drain. While noodles cook and cool, mix together lemon juice, oil, Accent and seasoning salt. Place into a large zip-close bag with noodles. Refrigerate overnight. Remove from refrigerator; add celery, onion, pepper, olives and mayonnaise. Mix together before serving.

Carolyn Allen
Rock Falls

Meat & Seafood

Simple Round Steak and Gravy

1 tablespoon margarine
1 round steak, cut into individual servings
1 (1-ounce) envelope onion soup mix
1 (10.75-ounce) can cream of chicken or cream of mushroom soup
1 cup water

Preheat oven to 450°. Use margarine to grease a 9x13-inch glass baking pan. Arrange round steak pieces in bottom of pan. Sprinkle with onion soup mix. Blend cream of chicken soup and water together; pour over steak. Cover; bake 15 minutes. Reduce heat to 375°; bake 1 hour and 15 minutes more. As it bakes, the gravy will form. Check on it 2 to 3 times while baking; add water as needed. This is yummy served with rice or mashed potatoes.

Allyn House

The Allyn House

1400 Mulholland Street • Nauvoo, IL 62354
217-453-2204 • www.allynhouseinnauvoo.com

The Allyn House, in uptown Nauvoo, showcases souvenirs and home décor that reflects the 1840's theme of the restored homes and businesses in Old Nauvoo. You will find more than 100 custom-made Nauvoo souvenirs available for sale as well as home décor items from Irvin's Tinware; Willow Tree Figures; Rowe Pottery; Manual Woodworkers and Weavers afghans and wall hangings; Park Designs dish towels, aprons, and rag rugs; Naked Bee lotions and soap; and Blossom Bucket signs and shelf decorations. In our back room is a replicated woodworker's shop reminiscent of the 1800's complete with tools and accessories. On display are examples of windows made by the late Charles W. Allen, using the mortise-and-tenon square peg joinery technique. Don't miss renowned watercolor artist Al Rounds' art gallery featuring scenes of Nauvoo. We love to greet visitors with a friendly hello as they come in to explore our little shop.

December–March: 10:00 am to 5:00 pm
March–May: 9:00 am to 6:00 pm
June–August: 9:00 am to 8:00 pm
September–November: 9:00 am to 6:00 pm

The Perfect Chicago-Style Hot Dog

1 all-beef frankfurter, roasted
1 poppy seed bun, heated
Yellow mustard
Onion, chopped
Sweet pickle relish, bright green
Dill pickle spear
Tomato slice or wedge
Pickled sport peppers
Celery salt

Place frankfurter in bun, top with mustard, onion and relish. Top with a dill spear along with tomato, peppers and a dash of celery salt. This process is also known as being "dragged through the garden" due to the many fresh toppings on the hot dog. The number 1 rule, however, is NEVER put ketchup on a Chicago Dog. Why is that? You will need to call Gilbert to find out!

The Chicago Tour Company

✶ ✶ ✶ ✶ ✶ THE
CHICAGO
TOUR COMPANY

4835 West Grace Street • Chicago, IL 60641
773-930-3710 • Fax: 773-930-3920
www.chicagotourco.com • Find us on Facebook

We Plan Everything For You!

Explore the Windy City with the Chicago Tour Company. Whether you are looking for a full, custom-designed itinerary, or need a local Chicago guide to show you around, the Chicago Tour Company is here for you!

Your group is in good hands with what is sure to become your go-to tour company in Chicago.

Choose from a variety of different themed tours, whether you want a general overview of Chicago or something more focused, such as a chocolate tour, church tour, cultural neighborhood tour, foodie tour, and many others.

Call The Chicago Tour Company today and create the perfect itinerary for your group!

Photography by www.GerardoM.com

Red Wine Braised Brisket

4 large garlic cloves
4 sprigs fresh rosemary, needles stripped and chopped
¼ cup extra-virgin olive oil, divided
1 (4-pound) beef brisket, first-cut
½ teaspoon kosher salt, plus more for seasoning
Coarsely ground black pepper
4 large carrots, 3-inch chunks
3 celery stalks, 3-inch chunks
4 large red onions, halved
2 cups dry red wine
1 (16-ounce) can whole tomatoes, hand crushed
1 handful fresh flat-leaf parsley leaves
3 bay leaves
1 tablespoon all-purpose flour, optional)

Preheat oven to 325°. On a cutting board, mash garlic into a paste using the flat side of a knife. Add rosemary and continue to mash until incorporated; transfer to a small bowl. Add 2 tablespoons olive oil; stir to combine. Season both sides of brisket with a fair amount of kosher salt and ground black pepper. Place a large roasting pan or Dutch oven over medium-high flame; coat with remaining olive oil. Put brisket in pan; sear both sides to a nice brown crust. Add vegetables around brisket; pour paste over top. Add wine and tomatoes; toss in parsley and bay leaves. Cover pan tightly with aluminum foil; transfer to oven. Bake 3 to 4 hours, basting every 30 minutes with pan juices, until beef is fork tender. Remove brisket to a cutting board; rest 15 minutes. Scoop vegetables out of pan; place on a platter. Cover; keep warm in oven. Pour off excess fat; place pan on stove over medium-high heat; boil 5 minutes, stirring constantly until sauce is reduced by half. (If you want a thicker sauce, mix 1 tablespoon flour with 2 tablespoons wine or water; blend into sauce).

Jeff Shapiro, Real Urban Barbecue
Little Bear Ribfest

Little Bear Ribfest

Mid-August

1001 Lakeview Parkway • Vernon Hills, IL 60061
847-996-6800 • www.vhparkdistrict.org

Vernon Hills Park District's annual Little Bear Ribfest cooks up a mix of blues, brews, and BBQ. Relax by Little Bear Lake in picturesque Century Park as you listen to the best live blues music and enjoy award-winning ribs and cold beer. Thank you to Vernon Hills' own Real Urban BBQ for providing these tasty recipes. Their famous burnt ends, award-winning ribs, pulled pork, turkey, brisket, and chicken have been a part of Ribfest since its conception. If you can't make it to Ribfest, be sure to stop in at one of their four locations in the Chicago area. Visit www.RealUrbanBBQ. com. Vernon Hills Park District addresses the lifelong leisure needs of all Vernon Hills residents. Our mission is to promote diverse community-based recreational opportunities by providing a variety of programs, services, facilities, and natural spaces to enhance the quality of life for our residents.

Chicago Italian Beef

3 cups water
1 teaspoon salt
1 teaspoon black pepper
1 sprig fresh oregano
1 sprig fresh basil
1 teaspoon onion salt
2 cloves fresh garlic
1 beef bouillon cube

1 (1-ounce) package Italian
   salad dressing mix
1 (5-pound) rump roast
1 rib celery, chopped
1 small onion, chopped
½ red bell pepper, sliced
1 package mushrooms, sliced
Italian rolls, toasted

In a saucepan over medium-high heat, combine water, salt, black pepper, oregano, basil, onion salt, garlic, bouillon cube and salad dressing mix. Stir well; bring to a boil. Place roast in a slow cooker; pour mixture over roast. Cover; cook on low 10 to 12 hours. In a small skillet, sauté celery, onion, bell pepper and mushrooms. Shred meat with a fork; serve on Italian rolls topped with sautéed vegetables.

Belvidere Park District

Belvidere Park District

The Historic Baltic Mill

1006 West Lincoln Avenue • Belvidere, IL 61008
815-547-5711 • www.belviderepark.org

The Belvidere Park District provides a backdrop of calming greenery as a natural setting for couples who want an outdoor celebration of their wedding day. They offer four wedding packages to choose from according to what the bride and groom would like. Each package offers a three-hour time block for ceremonies in an area with a stage and hillside seating for guests on natural limestone. Larger packages include a conference room and rehearsal time for the night before. Need an on-site wedding coordinator? All packages include one. This is on a first-come, first-served basis with various times available both weekends and daily. Bookings should be made at least ninety days in advance, but if available, accommodations may be made for any last minute requests. Call today to set up a tour and plan your special day.

Meatballs with Rhubarb Sauce

Sauce:

2 cups chopped rhubarb
½ cup water
1 cup brown sugar
1 (15-ounce) can tomato sauce
2 teaspoons molasses
¼ cup barbecue sauce

In a saucepan over medium heat, cook rhubarb with water until thick. Add brown sugar, tomato sauce and molasses; stir well. Stir in barbecue sauce. Simmer 15 minutes.

Meatballs:

1 pound ground beef
1 teaspoon salt
1 teaspoon garlic salt
16 Ritz crackers, crushed
¼ cup Rhubarb Sauce

Preheat oven to 350°. In a bowl, combine all ingredients; roll into 1-inch balls. Brown meatballs in oil; drain. Add meatballs to 2-quart casserole dish; pour Sauce on top. Bake 30 minutes. Sauce is also good on pork chops.

Mary Schrock, Winner, Condiments Category
Aledo Rhubarb Festival

Aledo Rhubarb Festival

1st Friday and Saturday in June

Aledo's Central Park ● 211 Southeast 3rd Street ● Aledo, IL 61231
309-582-7985 ● www.aledorhubarbfest.com

The Aledo Rhubarb Festival is a celebration of all things rhubarb—from pie to soda pop. If it's rhubarb, it's here. Aledo's affinity for rhubarb became official when the town of 3,600 was named the Rhubarb Capital of Illinois by Governor Pat Quinn. The unique festival, which is free to attend, draws nearly 10,000 visitors to the Mercer County seat. The festival is easy to find—at the crossroads of Illinois Highways 17 and 94—at Aledo's Central Park and the Mercer County Courthouse lawn. Since the festival began in 1991, the centerpiece attractions have always been the rhubarb tasting tent and the rhubarb pie. On Friday and Saturday, in the Big Blue Tent, festival goers may sample many rhubarb treats. Local non-profit organizations will be selling more than 3,000 rhubarb pies and rhubarb baked goods. Aledo Main Street will distribute 12,000 free seeds to festival visitors.

Red Fusion Sauce with Meatballs

Use your favorite meatballs with this rich sauce for a mouthwatering dish that is easy to make and can be served as a party appetizer or for a family dinner.

2 tablespoons olive oil
2 shallots, diced
1 garlic clove, minced
1½ tablespoons flour
2½ cups Vigneto del Bino Red Fusion
1 cup beef stock
1½ teaspoons sugar
1 (3-inch) rosemary sprig
Salt and fresh ground pepper to taste

Heat olive oil in a medium saucepot over medium heat. Add shallots and garlic; sauté until shallots are translucent. Sprinkle flour over top; stir until shallots are completely coated. Slowly pour in Red Fusion wine, stirring until smooth. Stir in stock. Add sugar and rosemary sprig. Add salt and pepper to taste. Simmer 20 to 25 minutes, stirring often. Preheat oven to 350°. Arrange meatballs in a lightly greased baking dish. Strain sauce through a fine strainer; pour over meatballs. Bake 15 to 17 minutes.

Vigneto del Bino Vineyard and Winery

Vigneto del Bino
Vineyard and Winery

Mid-March to end of December

42150 Crawford Road • Antioch, IL 60002
847-204-7352 • www.vignetodelbino.com

Vigneto del Bino Winery is a boutique winery specializing in "Wines Grown from Local Vines." American and French-hybrid grape varietals are also prominent in the vineyard. The winery building encompasses the manufacturing of the wines, a tasting room and gift shop. Relax and shop for gift items while sampling our crisp and refreshing wine selection. Along with wine-related gift items, we feature handmade items from local artists including wreaths made from our own vines. We are pleased to announce that Johnny's Chophouse restaurant in Antioch is featuring some of our wines. Stop by and enjoy their delicious foods paired with our award-winning wines.

Thursday & Sunday: Noon to 5:00 pm
Friday & Saturday: Noon to 7:00 pm

Grandma Slagel's BBQ

2 pounds ground beef
Salt and pepper to taste
2 tablespoons chopped onion
⅔ cup chopped celery
½ cup vinegar
½ cup brown sugar
½ cup tomato juice
3 tablespoons liquid mustard
2 tablespoons flour

In a skillet, brown ground beef, salt, pepper, onion and celery; drain. Add remaining ingredients; simmer over low heat until thick.

LouisJohn Slagel's Favorite Dish
Slagel Family Farm

-the Natural Choice in Quality meats-

Slagel Family Farm

June to October

23601 East 600 North Road • Fairbury, IL 61739
815-657-8160 • 815-848-9385 • www.slagelfamilyfarm.com

What better way is there to learn more about the food we eat than to come directly to the farm and see how it is grown and cared for? Slagel Family Farm is a sixth-generation family farm in central Illinois that is now inviting the public to join them on a farm tour of their old-fashioned livestock farm. Reconnect with the land and watch livestock roaming pastures under wide-open skies outside the city. As more and more people have the desire to learn more about their food and where it comes from, we felt offering a farm tour and dinner would be an excellent way to bring you closer to your food.

Apple Cider Stew

3 tablespoons flour
1 teaspoon salt
½ teaspoon pepper
1 pound beef stew meat, sliced into 1-inch pieces
2 tablespoons vegetable oil
2 cups apple cider
½ cup water
1 tablespoon vinegar
1 tablespoon brown sugar
½ teaspoon dried thyme
1 stalk celery, cut into ½-inch lengths
1 medium onion, chopped
1½ cups chopped carrots
3 cups chopped potatoes

In a large plastic bag, combine flour, salt and pepper; shake to mix. Add beef and toss to coat. In a large saucepan, heat oil. Add beef and cook until browned. Add cider, water, vinegar, brown sugar and thyme; bring to a boil. Reduce heat and simmer 30 minutes. Add celery and onion; simmer 30 more minutes. Add carrots and potatoes. Continue to simmer another 30 minutes or until vegetables are tender.

Stade's Farm and Market

Stade's Farm and Market

3709 Miller Road • McHenry, IL 60051

815-675-6396 • www.stadesfarmandmarket.com • Find us on Facebook

Located approximately fifty miles northeast of Chicago in scenic McHenry County, Stade's Farm and Market raises crops ranging from traditional corn and soybeans to specialty crops as well as many fruits and vegetables commonly grown in the Midwest. Stade's offers a wide variety of fruits and vegetables for u-pick, beginning with strawberries in June and ending with pumpkins and apples in October. Stade's has a full-service market, including a bakery. In addition to homegrown, delicious produce, they offer many artisan products, including honey produced by bees on location. Stade's fall harvest festival, Shades of Autumn, features unique family-friendly entertainment, special events, pumpkin and apple picking, and hayrides for you to enjoy with your loved ones while surrounded by the sights and sounds autumn has to offer. Weekly Christian contemporary worship services are held every Sunday morning, Memorial Day weekend through October.

June–December
9:00 am to 6:00 pm

Burgoo Stew

¾ cup soy sauce
1 cup Merlot
2 tablespoons minced garlic
2 tablespoons chopped onion
3 tablespoons black pepper
3 pounds beef stew meat
1½ cups olive oil

1 cup chopped carrots
1 cup chopped celery
2 pounds potatoes, chopped
2 cups frozen corn
1 yellow onion, chopped
4½ (14-ounce) cans stewed tomatoes
1 (32-ounce) box beef stock

Combine soy sauce, Merlot, garlic, onion and pepper in a large sealable container; mix well. Add stew meat; refrigerate 24 hours. In a large stockpot over medium heat, heat olive oil; add meat and marinade. Turn heat to low and simmer 1 hour. Add carrots, celery, potatoes, corn and onion; simmer 2 hours. Add tomatoes and beef stock; simmer 1 hour. Enjoy!

Burgoo Festival
LaSalle County Historical Society

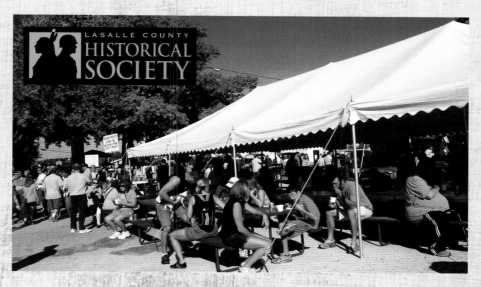

Burgoo Festival

Columbus Day Weekend

101 East Canal Street • Utica, IL 61373
815-667-4861 • www.lasallecountyhistoricalsociety.org

Started in 1969, Burgoo Festival is the main fundraiser for the LaSalle County Historical Society. This pioneer stew is slow cooked every year over an open fire overnight by the Burgoomeister and served to festivals attendees on the Sunday of the festival. Be sure to visit this family-friendly event and enjoy a sample of Burgoo Stew as you shop more than 350 vendors in quaint downtown Utica, Illinois.

Saturday: 11:00 am to 6:00 pm
Sunday: 9:00 am to 5:00 pm

Families Guinness Stew

2 pounds boneless lamb, cubed (may substitute beef sirloin)
Salt and pepper to taste
Flour for dredging
4 tablespoons unsalted Kerrygold Irish butter
¼ cup canola or olive oil
4 medium onions, chopped
2 cups low-sodium beef broth
2 cups Guinness stout (keep a couple extra bottles handy)
5 carrots, peeled and thickly sliced
4 parsnips, peeled and thickly sliced
1 medium turnip, peeled and cut into 1-inch pieces
Mashed or boiled potatoes

Season meat with salt and pepper; dredge in flour. In a stockpot, melt butter and oil. Working in batches, brown meat on all sides 5 to 7 minutes or until evenly browned. Remove from pot. Stir in onions; cook 3 to 5 minutes until soft. Return meat to pot; add broth and Guinness to cover. Bring to a boil; reduce heat to medium low. Cover; simmer 60 to 70 minutes. When meat is almost tender, add carrots, parsnips and turnip; cook 30 to 40 minutes until vegetables and meat are tender and stew is thickened. Ladle stew into shallow bowls with a scoop of potatoes.

Naperville Bites and Sites

Naperville Bites and Sites

Last Weekend in March to 1st Weekend in December

Tours Start: 5th Avenue • Naperville, IL 60563
630- 347-6553 • www.napervillefoodtours.com

Naperville Bites and Sites is a food tasting and historical walking tour of downtown Naperville. Enjoy a culinary and cultural walking experience through Naperville's historic neighborhood, one delicious taste at a time. Experience and discover fabulous food tastings from specialty food stores, hidden works of art, sculpture, and murals throughout the walk of beautiful downtown Naperville.

Pathfinder Chili

Every year during the second weekend in October, OnTarget Range hosts the Great Chili Cookoff where our customers and employees submit their finest chili to be judged by all other customers leaving our range. The winner receives a plaque and range passes and our OnTarget charity of the quarter receives all the donations made by our customers, who are asked to donate cash to their favorite chili. The winner is the cook with the most amount of donations at the end of the day. It is a festive occasion, and the chili contestants surround a bonfire in our parking lot. Donations are not mandatory. The OnTarget Director always submits his Pathfinder Chili that has won chili contests at two different US embassies: Bogota, Colombia and Amman, Jordan.

5 pounds ground meat (beef, deer or elk)
2 tablespoons butter
1 large Spanish onion, chopped
2 red bell peppers, chopped
3 poblano peppers, chopped
2 habenero peppers, chopped
4 jalapeño peppers, chopped, 2 left whole for aesthetic appeal
2 (1.75-ounce) packages chili powder
1 teaspoon cumin
2 (15-ounce) cans black beans
2 (15-ounce) cans red kidney beans
3 (15-ounce) cans crushed tomatoes (or equivalent fresh tomatoes)
1 (15-ounce) can whole-kernel corn
2 tablespoons liquid smoke
1 tablespoon Worchestershire sauce
1 tablespoon white vinegar
2 tablespoons sugar
Salt and pepper to taste

In a large stockpot over medium-high heat, brown meat in butter just until no longer pink. Add onion, chopped peppers, whole jalapeños, chili powder and cumin; cook until vegetables are tender. Add beans, tomatoes, corn, liquid smoke and Worcestershire; simmer 1 hour. Add vinegar and sugar; cook 15 minutes more. Taste before adding salt and pepper; cook another 15 minutes. Best served over white rice.

Tom Dorsch, Director of Operations
OnTarget Range & Tactical Training Center

OnTarget Range & Tactical Training Center

560 Beechcraft Lane • Crystal Lake, IL 60012
815-477-2020 • www.ontargetsite.com • Find us on Facebook

OnTarget Range & Tactical Training Center is a state-of-the-art shooting range for pistols and rifles. The pro shop helps you find the perfect firearm, ammo and gear for your needs. Under the compassionate guidance of seasoned instructors, they offer introductory through expert firearm classes for the entire family. Everyone is welcome at the range–from first-time shooters to experts looking to maintain or improve their skills. All rifles up to a fifty caliber are welcome on our fifty-yard range while handgun shooters can enjoy our 25 yard range. Both ranges have twelve shooting lanes each and are equipped with the finest ventilation system in the industry. If you are a firearm enthusiast looking for an enjoyable and educational experience, visit OnTarget, "Your Resource for Shooting Excellence." Check out the perks of becoming a member.

Monday–Saturday: 9:00 am to 8:00 pm
Sunday: 9:00 am to 6:00 pm

You don't have to be a member to enjoy the facilities. However, membership does have its perks: Reduced Rates • Priority Scheduling • Guest Passes and more. Special rates for Seniors, First Responders, and Active Duty/Retired Military.

Ann's Wild Stinging Nettle and Ramp White Chicken Chili

2 (8-ounce) chicken breasts
1 teaspoon salt
½ teaspoon black pepper
8 ounces smoky country ham (preferably Benton's brand), julienned
1 large red bell pepper, julienned
10 wild leeks or ramps, washed and thinly sliced
3 cloves garlic, thinly sliced
1 small bunch wild garlic mustard (or broccoli raab), washed and roughly sliced
2 leaves wild garlic mustard or stinging nettles (or kale from the store), washed, destemmed and rough chopped
2 cups white wine
16 dashes hot sauce (something thick and vinegary like Cholula)
1 stick butter
1 (15-ounce) can large butter beans, drained
3 teaspoons red wine vinegar
½ teaspoon ground cumin
¼ teaspoon ground coriander

Preheat oven to 400°. Season chicken breasts with salt and pepper. In a large saucepot over medium-high heat, sear chicken on both sides until golden brown. Remove pot from heat and set aside (without washing). Place chicken in a baking dish and cover half way with hot water. Cover with foil and bake 30 minutes while completing recipe. Add ham to reserved pot and place over medium-high heat; cook until ham is browned. Add bell pepper, leeks and garlic; sauté 2 minutes. Add wild garlic mustard and stir. Remove all to a bowl. Deglaze pan by adding white wine and hotsauce, stirring from the bottom to scrape pan. Pour over contents in bowl and add all back into pot while continuing to cook over medium heat. After 30 minutes of cook time, check chicken. When cooked through and tender, shred with 2 forks and then add to pot along with liquid. Add butter and reduce heat to medium low (to keep at a high simmer) and continue to cook until half the liquid is gone and chili begins to thicken. Add butter beans, red wine vinegar, cumin and coriander; mix well. Season to taste with additional salt if needed. Continue to cook just until beans are heated through.

Chef Ann Swanson
for Allerton Park & Retreat Center

Allerton Park & Retreat Center

515 Old Timber Road • Monticello, IL 61856
217-333-3287 • www.allerton.illinois.edu

Built in 1900 as a private residence by artist and philanthropist Robert Allerton, Allerton Park and Retreat Center offers a unique opportunity to experience art, nature, and history away from the distractions of everyday life. Explore fourteen miles of hiking trails, wander through formal gardens with over one hundred garden ornaments, marvel at the century-old mansion, and find peace in the quiet, expansive grounds. Allerton has become a destination for meetings, conferences, weddings, retreats, and special events for people from all over the country. Organized programs open to the community and visitors include outdoor concerts, youth summer camps, themed dinners and educational events, nature hikes, and public tours. Overnight accommodations are available. Entrance is free.

"This place has a little magic for every person who visits." —excerpt from a review of Allerton.

Open Year-Round • 8:00 am to Sunset
Visitor Center: 9:00 am to 5:00 pm

Grilled Chicken Horseshoe Sandwich

The Horseshoe is an open-faced sandwich created in 1920 in Springfield, Illinois, by Chef Joe Schweska of the Leland Hotel. It is a local favorite that people will drive miles for just to indulge in the decadent cheese-covered dish. It consists of thick-sliced toasted bread—often Texas toast—a hamburger patty, French fries, and a "secret" cheese sauce. Common replacements for the hamburger patty include ham, deep-fried pork tenderloin, grilled or fried chicken breast, and fried fish fillets. Local eateries pride themselves on their version of the secret cheese sauce. Here's a recipe from a Springfield local who thinks they have cracked the code.

1 (9-ounce) bag frozen crinkle-cut French fries
4 boneless chicken breasts, halved
1 teaspoon garlic salt
2 teaspoons Cavendar's Greek seasoning
½ cup butter
¼ cup all-purpose flour
2 cups half-and-half
2 teaspoons Worcestershire
3 ounces full-bodied beer
2 cups shredded Cheddar cheese
Salt and ground black pepper to taste
4 slices bread (or garlic toast), toasted
Hot sauce, blue cheese or ranch dressing, for dipping

Preheat oven to 400°. Spread French fries on a baking sheet. Bake 20 minutes or until golden brown. While fries are baking, rub chicken breasts with garlic salt and Cavendar's. Fry chicken breasts on grill or in a large skillet over medium-high heat until done (about 4 minutes per side). Melt butter in saucepan over medium heat and whisk in flour; cook, stirring constantly, 4 minutes to remove flavor of raw flour. Gradually whisk in half-and-half, Worcestershire and beer so that no lumps form. Bring to a simmer; remove from heat and add cheese, stirring until melted. Season with salt and pepper. Place 2 slices toasted bread onto 2 dinner plates; top each slice with a grilled chicken breast. Top each breast with French fries; pour cheese sauce over top. Serve immediately. Provide side dishes of hot sauce, blue cheese or ranch to dip your Horseshoe in.

Springfield Park District

 **Springfield Park District**

Where You Can Play, Your Way, Everyday!

Springfield Park District

2500 South 11th Street • Springfield, IL 62703
217-544-1751 • www.springfieldparks.org

The Springfield Park District was organized in February 1900, the second park district established in the state of Illinois. Its boundaries encompass the greater portion of the Springfield metropolitan area, covering approximately sixty square miles, 2,500 acres, thirty-four parks, recreation facilities, thirteen miles of bike trails, four golf courses, and even a zoo. The Springfield Park District is a place for visitors to "play their way, every day." Plan to visit their Nelson Center Ice Arena, historical Washington Park, Henson Robinson Zoo, and so much more.

Southwind Park is Springfield's most inclusive attraction and sets a new national standard, not just for accessibility, but also for environmental excellence. Erin's Pavilion, which is a premiere rental facility and serves as the welcome and visitors center, is a Platinum LEED-certified building, and many features throughout the eighty-acre park exceed ADA accessibility requirements. Other eco-friendly features include wetlands, a wind turbine, solar panels, and a geothermal system. Come play on the two largest playgrounds in the district, and frolic all day in the hot sun at our Splash Pad.

Open since 1970, the Springfield Park District's Henson Robinson Zoo offers visitors a glance at native and exotic animals in a park-like setting. The zoo is home to animals from Africa, Asia, Australia, and North and South America. Come out for a picnic, see all the animals, and ride the Zoo Train.

Go to the Springfield Park District website to find contact info and hours of operation for all of our parks and facilities.

Vietnamese Pork Banh Mi

Pork:

2 teaspoons cooking oil
1 pound ground pork
2 cloves garlic, minced
2 green onions, minced
**2 tablespoons fish sauce (Asian section of most grocery stores or substitute
    Worcestershire sauce)**
1½ tablespoons Sriracha hot sauce
17 leaves fresh basil, divided
6 French or Italian sub rolls
3 to 4 sprigs cilantro

Heat oil over medium-high heat in a large skillet. Add pork; stir to break up. When
pork just starts to brown, add garlic and onions; stir to combine. Add fish sauce and
Sriracha; cook until meat starts to darken. Remove from heat; stir in 5 leaves chopped
basil. Open rolls; place pork inside. Add Sriracha Mayonnaise and Pickled Vegetables.
Add 2 basil leaves and cilantro sprig to each sandwich.

Sriracha Mayonnaise:

¾ cup mayonnaise
½ cup Sriracha

In a small bowl, combine mayonnaise and Sriracha.

Pickled Vegetables:

¼ cup rice wine vinegar (or white vinegar)
¼ cup sugar
½ cup water
1 cup peeled and julienned Daikon radish (or jicama)
1 cup peeled and julienned carrot

In a medium-sized saucepan over medium heat, combine vinegar, sugar, water and
vegetables; bring to a boil. When sugar is dissolved reduce heat to low; gently simmer
5 to 10 minutes to pickle vegetables. Remove vegetables from syrup mixture; allow to
cool slightly.

Chicago Foodways Tours

Chicago Foodways Tours

312-203-4767 • www.chicagofoodways.com

If America is a melting pot, Chicago is the rich stew it produced. Since the city's founding, wave after wave of immigrants have come to claim their territories, make their fortunes, and leave their mark. Those marks are the quilt squares that make up this City of Neighborhoods. Beyond the gleaming skyscrapers and bustling Loop lies a grid of small towns, strung together by the same city streets, but set apart by different flavors, characters, and architectural landmarks. Chicago Foodways takes you into the neighborhoods. You'll meet the mom and pop owners of small markets, restaurants, bakeries, and taverns. Get an understanding of why people from all over the world settled into various parts of the city, and best of all, taste the foods they brought with them!

Cheesy Corn and Sausage Stuffed Ravioli

Dough:

3 cups flour
3 eggs
1½ tablespoons oil
6 to 7 tablespoons water

Combine all ingredients in a bowl, mix until dough forms. Divide into 2 equal portions. Refrigerate at least 3 hours.

Filling:

6 ears fresh sweet corn, kernels removed
¾ pound pork sausage, browned and drained
1 cup shredded Asiago cheese
½ cup shredded mozzarella cheese
½ cup grated Parmesan cheese
1 (15-ounce) carton ricotta cheese

Mix all ingredients together; set aside. Roll first dough portion to ¹⁄₁₆-inch thick (very thin). Press a ravioli form (or cookie cutter) lightly into dough to mark raviolis (do not cut through). Place 1 tablespoon filling onto center of each ravioli. Roll second dough to ¹⁄₁₆-inch thick and same dimensions as first. Place over filling-topped dough and cut with ravioli form. Place on a floured cookie sheet until all are cut. Cook in salted boiling water 3 to 4 minutes. Top with Roasted Red Pepper and Basil Sauce.

Roasted Red Pepper and Basil Sauce:

2 tablespoons minced garlic
¼ cup chopped fresh basil
3 tablespoons olive oil
2 large red bell peppers, roasted and seeded
2 cups half-and-half
4 tablespoons butter

In a skillet, sauté garlic and basil in oil until tender; add to blender. Purée red bell peppers in blender with garlic and basil. Return to skillet and bring to a light boil. Reduce heat to simmer. Stir in half-and-half and butter; continue stirring until butter melts. Simmer 5 minutes. Serve over Cheesy Corn and Sausage Stuffed Ravioli.

Mendota Sweet Corn Festival

Mendota Sweet Corn Festival

2nd Weekend in August

Downtown • Mendota, IL 61342
815-539-6507 • www.sweetcornfestival.com

The good times are waiting and the welcome mat is out for one of the Midwest's oldest and largest harvest festivals—Mendota Sweet Corn Festival. Experience a true family festival sponsored by the Mendota Chamber of Commerce. You'll enjoy free musical entertainment, the Crafter's Market Place and Flea Market, Queen Pageant, parade, carnival with rides for both adults and children, and food booths featuring a multitude of ethnic, regional, and festival foods. Don't miss the "Big Event" on Sunday afternoon—the serving of tons of free hot, buttered, delicious Del Monte sweet corn. For more than sixty-eight years, the corn has been cooked to its golden goodness with the help of a vintage steam engine. The Chamber sells fresh Del Monte corn by the bag during the festival. Be sure to get your share of the sweet buttered corn offered while visiting this fun family event.

Deer Roast

3 tablespoons butter
1 (3½-pound) venison roast
1 (1.9-ounce) package Lipton onion soup mix
2½ cups water
1 teaspoon chopped thyme
1 cup dry red wine, optional
Salt and pepper to taste

In a skillet, melt butter; brown roast on all sides. Place roast in roaster pan. In a bowl, combine remaining ingredients; mix well. Pour over roast; cover. Bake at 350° for 2 hours or until tender.

Steve Phelps
Illinois Trophy Bowhunters

Illinois Trophy Bowhunters Inc.

520 Juniper Drive • Petersburg, IL 62675
217-632-4595 • 217-414-4471
www.illinoistrophybowhuntersinc.com

If you want to bowhunt Illinois, your search for an Illinois bowhunting outfitter is over. Illinois Trophy Bowhunters have been bowhunting the state since 1991. As one of the oldest Illinois whitetail deer hunting outfitters, you can rest assured ITB has figured out how to successfully bowhunt Illinois so you have an outstanding hunting experience. While bowhunting is the core of the operation, they also offer a select number of whitetail gun hunts during the firearm deer season. Illinois Trophy Bowhunters are avid hunters and know the specific requirements needed to successfully bowhunt Illinois because that is all they do. Illinois is the only state they hunt and trophy whitetail deer is the only animal they are after. "Where Whitetail Dreams Come True" is not only ITB's slogan, but is their mission statement as well. Illinois Trophy Bowhunters have fine-tuned every aspect of your deer hunt to maximize your chance of bowhunting success.

Book your Illinois Deer Hunt Today so we can make YOUR "Whitetail Dreams Come True!"

Baked Atlantic Salmon with Pesto

2 (8-ounce) fresh Atlantic salmon fillets
White wine
1 lemon, halved
Kosher salt
Black pepper
Pesto

Preheat oven to 450°. Place salmon fillets, skin side down, on a small cooking sheet. Add white wine to cover bottom of cooking sheet; squeeze fresh lemon juice over salmon. Sprinkle kosher salt and black pepper over fillets; bake 10 minutes. Spread pesto on top; bake an additional 3 minutes. Plate each salmon fillet; garnish with fresh pesto.

Acquaviva Winery

Acquaviva Winery

47 West 614 IL-38 • Maple Park, IL 60151
630-365-0333 • www.acquavivawinery.com

Acquaviva is a family-owned, forty-acre estate vineyard with a full-service restaurant and winery located at the corner of Route 38 and Meredith Road in Maple Park. The 20,000-square-foot facility includes a tasting bar and scheduled facility tours, Neapolitan-style pizza and delicious cuisine, retail marketplace, private event and wedding space, as well as a visible winemaking production center. Along with award-winning wines, Acquaviva also boasts a new guest house, amazing architecture and hand-painted fine art by world-renowned artist Andrew Zabela. The estate produces many grape varietals all perfectly suited to sustain and thrive through the turbulent Midwest seasons. These grapes include Prairie Star, Brianna, Chardonel, Marechal Fosh, and Frontenac, among other Illinois favorites. Over the past fifteen years, the Brandonisio family has selected and hand-planted vines and allowed them time to mature and flourish. This beautiful vineyard and winery is a must-see Illinois gem.

Tuesday–Thursday: 11:00 am to 9:00 pm
Friday & Saturday: 11:00 am to 10:00 pm
Sunday: Noon to 8:00 pm

Teriyaki with Sriracha Cream Sauce

½ cup reduced-sodium soy sauce
½ cup packed brown sugar
¼ teaspoon garlic powder
2 tablespoons honey
1¼ cups water, divided
1 tablespoon cornstarch

4 (5-ounce) salmon fillets
½ cup mayonnaise
2 tablespoons Sriracha sauce
1½ tablespoons sweetened
   condensed milk

In a small saucepan over medium heat, combine soy sauce, sugar, garlic powder, honey and 1 cup water; bring to a simmer. In a small bowl, whisk together cornstarch and ¼ cup water; add to soy mixture. Simmer, stirring constantly, until thick enough to coat back of spoon. Remove from heat; cool to room temperature. Marinate fillets at least 30 minutes, better overnight, turning occasionally.

Preheat oven to 400°. Lightly spray with cooking spray, an 8x8-inch baking dish; add fillets with marinade. Bake 20 minutes or until fish flakes. In another bowl, while fish cooks, mix together mayonnaise, Sriracha and condensed milk; set aside. Serve fillets with cream sauce. Serves 4.

City of Olney

Norwegian Fiskepudding
(Fish Pudding)

1 tablespoon soft butter
2 tablespoons dry breadcrumbs
1½ pounds cod or haddock, skinned and boned
1½ cups cream
2 teaspoons salt
1½ tablespoons cornstarch

Preheat oven to 350°. Using a pastry brush or paper towel, evenly cover a 1½-quart loaf pan (or similar mold) with butter. Sprinkle breadcrumbs over butter making sure crumbs are evenly distributed; gently tap off excess. Cut fish into small pieces. Using a blender on high speed, purée about a third of the pieces, adding about a third of the cream for better puréeing; scrape sides and blend again to avoid chunks. Pour into a large mixing bowl. Repeat 2 more times until all fish is a smooth purée and has been added to mixing bowl. Add salt and cornstarch; beat until very light and fluffy. Pour into buttered pan; drop pan onto counter sharply to remove any air pockets. Smooth top with a spatula; seal with buttered sheet of foil. Place pan in a larger flat baking pan; add enough boiling water to come three quarters of the way up sides of bottom pan. Bake on middle rack 60 to 75 minutes checking frequently to ensure water simmers but does not boil. Fiskepudding is ready when top is firm to the touch and a toothpick (or fork) inserted into middle comes out dry and clean. Remove from oven; set aside 2 to 3 minutes. Pour off excess liquid (if any) and guide a sharp knife along edges. Put a heated plate on top of Fiskepudding and quickly invert. Pudding should easily come out of mold. Serve this delicious Fiskepudding while still hot.

Scandinavian Day Festival

Mr. Mounds' Crab Surprise

1 medium onion, chopped
1 tablespoon minced garlic
1 tablespoon butter (or olive oil)
1 (4-ounce) can sliced mushrooms
1 celery stalk, thinly sliced
1 (1-pound) package imitation crabmeat, bite-sized pieces
1 teaspoon curry powder
Salt and pepper to taste
1 to 2 cups prepared rice
3 tablespoons Miracle Whip (mayonnaise or sour cream)
1 tablespoon seasoned mustard
1 tablespoon lemon juice
1 teaspoon chopped basil leaves
¼ cup milk
2 tablespoons sherry (cream, dry, or cooking)
Grated Parmesan cheese to taste

In a large skillet over medium heat, sauté onion and garlic in butter until translucent; while continuing to cook, add mushrooms and celery. Turn heat to low; add crab pieces while continuing to stir. Add curry powder, salt and pepper to prepared rice. In a small mixing bowl, combine Miracle Whip, mustard, lemon juice, basil, milk and sherry; blend until smooth. Taste; check if salt and pepper are needed. Stir sauce into crab mixture; cook until all is thoroughly heated. Place rice on serving plates, spoon crab mixture on top and garnish with Parmesan cheese. Generous serving for 2 people or can be divided for 4 smaller servings. This recipe utilizes most components found in the kitchen. Other materials can be substituted.

Bill Iseminger
Cahokia Mounds

Cahokia Mounds State Historic Site

30 Ramey Street • Collinsville, IL 62234
618-346-5160 • www.cahokiamounds.org

Cahokia Mounds State Historic site is a UNESCO World Heritage Site and US National Historic Landmark. The site interprets the remains of a city that flourished here about AD 1050 to 1300. At its peak, the site was about five square miles in area, with 10,000 to 20,000 inhabitants, and about 120 earthen mounds of varying shapes and sizes, the largest of which, Monks Mound, is about 100 feet tall and fourteen acres in area. The site preserves 2200 of the original 4000 acres, including over 70 mounds. Today a world-class interpretive center, iPod tours, hiking trails, and year-round events preserve and interpret the Mississippian culture group that created America's first city.

Pan Seared Prawns with Coconut Kaffir Lime Risotto & Saffron Carrot Velouté

8 prawns
¾ cup canola or vegetable oil, divided
½ cup minced shallots, divided
½ cup chopped garlic, divided
6 carrots, roughly chopped
½ cup white dry wine
8 tablespoons melted butter
½ cup flour
3½ (14-ounce) cans chicken/vegetable stock, divided
1(16-ounce) bag Arborio rice
4 Kaffir lime leaves (or zest of 4 limes)
Salt and pepper
2 (4-ounce) cans coconut milk
⅔ cup heavy cream
2 thyme sprigs
Mint leaves for garnish

Shell prawns; rinse, dry and set aside. To prepare velouté, using a saucepan over low heat, heat ½ cup oil; add ¼ cup shallots, ¼ cup garlic and carrots. Cook until shallots are translucent; add wine and cook down. Add 4 tablespoons butter and flour alternately until roux is made. Add 1 can stock; simmer 15 minutes. In another large stockpot over low heat, heat ¼ cup oil. Add remaining garlic and shallots; cook until translucent. Add rice and zest; lightly toast, stirring occasionally, 2 minutes. Add remaining stock, salt and pepper to taste. Add coconut milk; turn up heat until it boils. Reduce to simmer; cook, covered, 10 to 12 minutes. In a skillet, heat remaining oil. Sear prawns, with fresh thyme sprigs, on both sides until seared evenly and golden brown. Turn off the heat, add remaining butter and baste; remove pan from heat or remove prawns from pan. Add salt to taste. Plate risotto (removing any remaining lime leaves). Place seared prawns on top; garnish with mint leaves. TIP: Kaffir lime leaves can be found at most Thai or Asian markets.

Executive Chef Clayton Danenberger
Danenberger Family Vineyards

Danenberger Family Vineyards

12341 Irish Road • New Berlin, IL 62670
217-488-6321 • www.dfv-wines.com

Danenberger Family Vineyards is more than an estate winery—it's an experience to share with family and friends, bringing people together in conversation and laughter. Labor in the vineyard ends in a bottled moment to enjoy and reminisce about for years to come. DFV's passion for grapes, wine, and food is a part of our lifestyle, and we love to share it. Winemaker Susan Sullivan Danenberger approaches her wines like pieces of art, painting with different flavors and aromas, letting the grape tell its story with its tannins and selecting yeasts and barrels to complete the dream. Executive Chef Clayton Danenberger and Chef De Cuisine Zac Leepper create Gastonomy Theater at DFV to complement their wines. DFV boasts international award-winning wines and an epic live music venue local to the Illinois area. Sip, Savor, and Share a love of Cabernet Franc and culinary excellence.

Thursday & Friday: Noon to 6:00 pm
Saturday: Noon to 8:00 pm
Sunday: 1:00 pm to 6:00 pm
Closed in February

Sweet Desire Steak Marinade

Perfect for the grill.

**½ cup Sweet Desire Bourbon Barrel Aged Mead
   (from Wild Blossom Meadery & Winery)**
½ cup amino acids
2 tablespoons olive oil
1 tablespoon Dijon mustard
¼ cup light brown sugar
2 garlic cloves, grated
1 teaspoon fresh ground pepper

Whisk ingredients together. To use marinade, pour over a 4- to 8-ounce steak. Turn steak to cover evenly with marinade. Cover and refrigerate overnight (or at least 4 hours), turning twice. Remove steaks from refrigerator while preheating grill. Grill to personal preference.

Wild Blossom Meadery

Wild Blossom Meadery & Winery

9030 South Hermitage • Chicago, IL 60620
773-840-4642 • www.wildblossommeadery.com
Find us on Facebook: WildBlossomChicago

Wild Blossom Meadery & Winery, a fixture in Chicago for more than twenty years, is not only the first Chicago winery, but is also the only meadery in Illinois. The meads are made with locally sourced ingredients, including honey produced in Wild Blossom's bee hives. Wild Blossom offers a mead club, beer and wine making classes, meadery tours and mead and wine tastings. The meadery is available for private and fundraising event rentals. As days open and hours are seasonal, please visit our website for current schedule.

Wednesday, Thursday & Friday: 3:00 pm to 7:00 pm
Saturday: Noon to 7:00 pm

Pheasant Hollow
"Red Razz" BBQ Sauce

1 cup Red Razz wine
1 cup ketchup
¾ cup brown sugar
1 teaspoon chili powder
1 teaspoon salt
½ teaspoon allspice
½ teaspoon black pepper
½ teaspoon crushed red pepper
¼ cup honey

Using a medium saucepan over medium heat, reduce Red Razz by half. Add ketchup, brown sugar, chili powder, salt, allspice, black pepper and red pepper; simmer 15 minutes. Remove from heat; add honey. Brush on ribs over low heat on grill; let glaze cover the ribs.

Pheasant Hollow Winery

Desserts & Other Sweets

Ice Cream Cake

Using brownie mix instead of baking a cake from scratch saves time and makes this dessert extra rich and chocolaty.

1 package brownie mix, plus ingredients to prepare per directions
1 pint strawberry ice cream
½ cup heavy cream
¼ cup chocolate sauce

Heat oven according to brownie mix package directions. Lightly coat 3 (6x3-inch-deep) round cake pans with cooking spray. Line pans with parchment paper; spray parchment. Prepare brownie batter according to package directions. Divide among prepared pans and bake until a wooden pick inserted in the middle comes out clean, 25 to 30 minutes. Cool completely in pans and then transfer to a work surface. Clean 1 of the pans and line with plastic wrap so that it hangs at least 3 inches over all sides. Transfer ice cream to a large bowl and mash until slightly soft and spreadable. Place 1 brownie layer in bottom of prepared pan. Spread half the ice cream on top. Top with another brownie layer and then remaining ice cream. Top with remaining layer of brownie. Freeze until set, at least 2 hours. When ready to serve, beat cream in a large bowl with an electric mixer until medium-stiff peaks form. Remove cake from pan and peel away plastic wrap. Transfer to a serving plate. Spoon cream on top and drizzle with chocolate sauce.

The Plush Horse

The Plush Horse

Palos Park's "Sweetest" landmark, serving ice cream for over 75 years

12301 South 86th Avenue • Palos Park, IL 60464
708-448-0550 • www.theplushhorse.com • Find us on Facebook

A stop at The Plush Horse is an absolute must while visiting Chicago. This nostalgic ice cream parlor has been serving homemade ice cream since 1937 and remains the oldest landmark in Palos Park, having become a legend in its own time. Nestled among mature trees, The Plush Horse features a brick courtyard on its west side, Adirondack chairs for quiet lounging on its east side, and a private room above the parlor for small groups to host birthday parties and other special events. There is no doubt you'll find a new favorite here. They carry over sixty-five flavors every day, all year round! Seasonal sorbets are offered as a dairy-free option. During holidays, enjoy pumpkin and egg nog ice cream. Summer fan favorites include peach, banana, and Italian lemonade, just to name a few. The Plush Horse covers the classics as well with frothing root beer floats, cherry-topped sundaes, and signature banana splits. Take the Challenge: thirty-seven mini scoops of homemade ice cream in one chilled bowl!

Seasonal Hours
Sunday: 11:00 am to 10:00 pm
Monday–Saturday: 8:00 am to 10:00 pm

Call or check the website for more information.

Black Forest Ice Cream Cake

We bake the cake fresh in house, but bake your favorite from a box, cool and freeze for one hour.

1 quart black cherry ice cream from The Brown Cow Ice Cream Parlor, slightly softened
1 (16-ounce) jar hot fudge sauce from The Brown Cow Ice Cream Parlor, divided
1 (9- or 10-inch) chocolate cake, frozen
1 (8-ounce) carton Cool Whip
12 maraschino cherries with stems

Line a 9- or 10-inch cake pan with plastic wrap. Fill with ice cream and half the fudge sauce. Freeze 2 hours (or overnight). Slice cake in half, lengthwise, to create 2 thinner cake rounds. Place 1 cake layer on a plate or 10-inch cardboard cake round. Pop ice cream from cake pan and remove plastic wrap (run bottom of cake pan under warm water to release ice cream easily from pan). Place on top of first cake layer. Place remaining cake layer on top to make an ice cream sandwich. Top with Cool Whip. Freeze for 30 minutes. Remove from freezer 5 to 10 minutes before serving. Warm remaining hot fudge sauce, drizzle over cake. Garnish with cherries.

The Brown Cow Ice Cream Parlor

The Brown Cow
Ice Cream Parlor

7347 Madison Street • Forest Park, IL 60130
708-366-7970 • www.browncowicecream.com

In 2004, Connie and husband, Matt, opened The Brown Cow Ice Cream Parlor, an old-fashioned soda fountain where they serve delectable treats with old-fashioned charm. The parlor serves amazing homemade ice cream, root beer, fresh-baked pies and cakes, locally roasted gourmet coffee drinks, ice cream cakes, and pies. Their private party room is perfect for your next celebration, or they can cater a sundae bar at your office, home, school, or block party. Visit and enjoy a sweet treat with them. They look forward to serving you!

Mary Todd Lincoln's White Cake

1 cup almonds
1 cup butter
2 cups sugar
3 cups flour
3 teaspoons baking powder
1 cup milk
6 egg whites
1 teaspoon vanilla extract
Powdered sugar

Preheat oven to 350°. Grease and flour a Bundt cake pan. Blanch almonds by placing them in boiling water for exactly 60 seconds. Drain immediately and rinse in cold water; set aside to dry. Cream butter and sugar. Sift flour and baking powder 3 times. Add to creamed butter and sugar, alternating with milk. Chop almonds in a food processor until they resemble a coarse flour; stir into batter and beat well. Beat egg whites until stiff and fold into batter. Stir in vanilla extract. Pour into prepared pan and bake 1 hour or until a toothpick inserted comes out clean. Turn out on a wire rack and cool. When cool, sift powdered sugar over top. A basic white frosting sprinkled with almonds was also popular.

Lincoln's Table by Donna D. McCreary;
adapted by Janice Cooke Newman
Visit Springfield, Illinois

Mary Todd Lincoln loved entertaining. Living in the state capitol and being married to a politician and popular lawyer meant there was always an event to attend or host. Mary's lively wit and Southern hospitality made her a popular hostess. She once held a party to which 500 people were invited. But as it rained that night and there was a society wedding in a nearby town, only 300 people came. While these were essentially social occasions, Mary used these events to study people. She considered herself a good judge of character and gave her husband tips, that he greatly appreciated, on dealing with people. Mary's main homemaking interest appeared to be cooking, especially making sweets. The cookbooks she purchased after getting married are in the Abraham Lincoln Presidential Library in Springfield. Her white almond cake was one of Mr. Lincoln's favorite desserts. She had brought the recipe from her favorite bakery in Lexington, Kentucky. Mary baked the white cake for Abraham Lincoln when they were courting, as a Springfield housewife, and when she was First Lady. Today, there are many versions of it, including the one listed above.

—National Park Service, Lincoln Home

Visit Springfield

Open Year-Round

Springfield Illinois Convention and Visitors Bureau
109 North 7th Street • Springfield, IL 62701
1-800-545-7300 • www.visitspringfieldillinois.com

No one brings Lincoln to life like Visit Springfield. Visit always legendary Springfield, for the most sites dedicated to the life of Abraham Lincoln. History comes alive in Springfield with living history programs all summer long. Travel the Mother Road, Historic Route 66, or tour the architectural splendor of the Dana-Thomas House–a Frank Lloyd Wright design. There is something for everyone in Mr. Lincoln's hometown. Enjoy fine dining, and farm to table, or the unexpected dining destination. Plus enjoy hundreds of events and discover multiple sites and attractions. Visit always legendary Springfield, Illinois, today.

Carrot Cake

2 cups sugar	1 cup chopped pecans, divided
2 cups flour	1½ cups salad oil
2 teaspoons baking soda	4 eggs, beaten
3 teaspoons cinnamon	1 tablespoon vanilla
1 teaspoon salt	3 cups grated carrots

Preheat oven to 350°. In a large bowl, combine sugar, flour, baking soda, cinnamon, salt and ¾ cup pecans; mix well. Add oil, eggs and vanilla; mix well. Add carrots; mix well. Pour into a greased 9x13-inch cake pan; bake 30 minutes or until done. Cool before frosting.

Frosting:

1 (8-ounce) package cream cheese, softened	1½ tablespoons vanilla
1 stick butter, softened	2 cups powdered sugar

Blend cream cheese, butter and vanilla together. Add powdered sugar; mix well. Spread over cooled cake.

Lion Dan Hanneman
Elburn Days

Elburn Days

3rd Weekend in August

All Wheel Car Show

1st Sunday in October

500 Filmore Street • Elburn, IL 60119
630- 365-6315 • www.elburnlions.com • Find us on Facebook

Welcome to Elburn Days. Help support Elburn Lions Club's largest charity event while enjoying a great time with family and friends. This event helps support charities such as glaucoma screening, guide dogs for the blind hearing impaired, juvenile diabetes research, and other programs to help the community. Members and their families donate hundreds of hours to make this three-day event a success. Enjoy a Friday night kick-off parade, carnival rides for all ages, crafts, food and commercial booths, 4-H show, RC car racing, tractor pull, and the pie baking competition. Get your feet muddy in the mud volleyball event. All donations are welcome. Come back first Sunday in October for the All-Wheel Car Show where you will see more than 300 cars and motorcycles compete for Best of the Best. Enjoy another fun family day with swap meet, craft shows, food provided by the Leo Club, (the youth division of Elburn Lions Club), music, and sporting events.

White Fruit Cake

2 sticks butter, softened
1½ cups sugar
7 eggs
3 cups self-rising flour
1 teaspoon baking powder
1 teaspoon lemon extract
1 teaspoon almond extract
1 teaspoon vanilla extract
1 pound candied cherries, chopped
1 pound candied pineapple, chopped
1 pound pecans, chopped

Preheat oven to 250°. Cream butter and sugar; add eggs 1 at a time. In another bowl, sift flour with baking powder; add to batter. Add extracts and mix well. By hand, fold in candied fruit and pecans. Bake in a greased tube pan 2½ hours or bake as drop cookies on baking sheet at 325°.

RiverBank Lodge

Open Year-Round

522 South 6th Street • Petersburg, IL 62675
217-632-0202 • www.riverbanklodge.com
Find us on Facebook

RiverBank Lodge is a beautiful and unique hotel located in the heart of historic Menard County on the banks of the Sangamon River in Petersburg. While providing the amenities of a modern and professionally managed hotel, RiverBank also provides the benefits of a smaller, locally owned and operated business. The beautiful lodge offers twenty-four guest rooms, on-site conference or banquet facilities, a gift shop, free wifi, and a full-service, cozy lounge where guests enjoy delicious homemade pizza, appetizers, and drinks. At RiverBank, there is something guests of all kinds will love, from the outdoorsman to the historical enthusiast, from antique shopper or golfer to wine connoisseur, to anyone just looking for an enjoyable getaway. Whether you are searching for a group gathering place or a romantic escape for two, you won't be disappointed by a visit to RiverBank Lodge. Take advantage of their outstanding service and hospitality. Plan your visit now.

Red Carpet Cupcakes

¾ cup unsalted butter, softened
2¼ cups sugar
3 large eggs, room temperature
2 tablespoons liquid red food coloring
3 tablespoons unsweetened cocoa powder
1½ teaspoons vanilla extract
1½ teaspoons salt
1½ cups buttermilk
3⅓ cups cake flour
1½ teaspoons white vinegar
1½ teaspoons baking soda

Preheat oven to 350°. Line a muffin tin with paper liners and spray with cooking spray; set aside. In bowl of a stand mixer, combine butter and sugar; mix on medium speed until very light and fluffy. Add eggs, 1 at a time, beating well after each addition. In a small bowl, whisk food coloring, cocoa powder and vanilla together; add to butter mixture, mixing well. Stir salt into buttermilk; add to batter in 3 parts, alternating with cake flour. In a small bowl, stir together vinegar and baking soda; add to batter, mixing well. Fill cupcake liners two-thirds full with batter; bake 17 to 18 minutes or until a toothpick inserted in center comes out clean. Do not overbake. Repeat with remaining cupcakes. Cool completely; top with Red Cream Cheese Frosting. Makes about 3½ dozen cupcakes.

Red Cream Cheese Frosting:

1 cup unsalted butter, softened
1 (8-ounce) package cream cheese, softened
¼ teaspoon salt
2 teaspoons vanilla extract
4½ cups powdered sugar
1 tablespoon milk (plus more if needed)
Red food coloring
Gold sprinkles, optional

In a large bowl, mix together butter, cream cheese, salt and vanilla until smooth. Add powdered sugar, 1 cup at a time, beating well after each addition. If frosting is too thick, add a little milk. Add a generous amount of food coloring to get a deep red hue. Pipe or spread onto each cooled cupcake; dust with gold sprinkles to finish it off.

The Orpheum Theatre

The Orpheum Theatre

57 South Kellogg Street • Galesburg, IL 61401

309-342-2299 • www.galesburgorpheum.org • Find us on Facebook

Described as "a veritable house of enchantment" when it opened its doors on August 21, 1916, the Orpheum Theatre continues to be a place of beauty and a showcase for the arts in western Illinois. Built as a vaudeville house, the Orpheum Theatre hosted many early stars of stage and screen, including Jack Benny, George Burns, Houdini, Al Jolson, Fanny Brice, and Blackstone the Magician. Today, the theatre continues to reflect its former glory, bringing to the stage a diverse blend of the finest entertainment in its flagship Red Carpet Series, educating students through the magic of theatre with its Youth Entertainment Series (YES), and offering free movies during the summer months with its Throwback Thursdays Summer Movie Series. The theatre is also home to many local performing arts and non-profit organizations that bring music, movies, dance, and theatre to its stage.

Monday–Friday: 10:00 am to 5:00 pm

Creamy Toffee Cheesecake

1½ cups graham cracker crumbs
¾ cup plus 3 tablespoons sugar, divided
⅓ cup butter, melted
4 (8-ounce) packages cream cheese, softened
½ cup packed light brown sugar
3 tablespoons flour
5 eggs, beaten
¼ cup sour cream
¼ cup heavy whipping cream
¼ cup boiled cider (or maple syrup)
1 cup R.G.W. English butter crunch toffee bits, divided, plus more for garnish

Preheat oven to 350°. Butter a 9-inch springform pan; wrap outside of pan with a double layer of foil. In a small mixing bowl, combine graham cracker crumbs, 3 tablespoons sugar and butter. Press firmly into bottom and 1 inch up sides of pan; set aside. In a large mixing bowl, beat cream cheese on high until smooth, approximately 5 minutes. Reduce speed to low, add remaining sugars and flour, mixing until smooth. Beat in eggs, sour cream, heavy cream and cider until just incorporated. Fold in ¾ cup toffee bits and pour batter into pan. Sprinkle top batter with remaining toffee bits. Place baking pan in a large roasting pan; fill roaster halfway up sides of springform pan with water. Bake 90 minutes or until middle is just set. Remove from water; cool on rack 30 minutes. Run a knife around edges to loosen; refrigerate until ready to serve. When ready to serve, place large toffee bits around edge and slice. Serves 10 to 12.

R.G.W. Candy Company

Photos by Nancy Rollings Saul

R.G.W. Candy Company

1865 2200th Street • Atlanta, IL 61723
309-830-4361 • Find us on Facebook

In the 1930's, brothers David and Bob Wertheim were quite well-known around central Illinois for being confectioners of new and delightfully tasty candies. Unfortunately, about 1934, they had a falling out over a young lady from Atlanta. Although the two brothers went their separate ways, David to Washington state and Bob to Atlanta to marry his sweetheart, both continued to dabble in candy-making. Around 1948, Robert G. (Bob) Wertheim officially started R.G.W. Candy Company, making his own confections and a few select items from recipes last published in 1908. His son, Tom Wertheim, continued the tradition for the second generation, and in 2016, Amy Wertheim, Bob's granddaughter, became the third generation to continue the legacy of only using the simplest ingredients required to make candy the way it used to be made—without preservatives, flavorings, modern chemistry, or machinery. R.G.W. Candy Company offers you "regular old candy", handmade and hand-dipped especially for you.

Monday–Saturday: 9:00 am to 4:00 pm
Sunday: 1:00 pm to 4:00 pm

Pecan-Strawberry Shortcakes

6 cups sliced fresh strawberries
¾ cup plus 2 tablespoons sugar, divided
1 tablespoon grated orange rind, divided
2 cups all-purpose flour
2 teaspoons baking powder
½ cup ground pecans
½ cup butter or margarine
⅔ cup milk
1 large egg, lightly beaten
1 cup whipping cream
½ teaspoon vanilla extract

Combine strawberries, ¼ cup sugar and 1 teaspoon orange rind in a large bowl; stir gently. Let stand at room temperature at least 20 minutes. Combine flour, baking powder, pecans and ½ cup sugar in a medium bowl; cut in butter with pastry blender until mixture is crumbly. Combine remaining orange rind, milk and egg; stir well. Add egg mixture to flour mixture, stirring just until dry ingredients are moistened. Drop batter evenly into 9 mounds on an ungreased baking sheet; flatten mounds slightly with back of a spoon to ¾-inch thickness. Bake at 450° for 8 to 9 minutes or until lightly browned. Let cool completely on a wire rack. Beat whipping cream until foamy; gradually add 2 tablespoons sugar and vanilla, beating until soft peaks form. Split shortcakes in half horizontally. Place bottom halves, cut side up, on individual dessert plates. Spoon half of strawberry mixture and half of whipped cream evenly over shortcake bottoms. Top each with remaining shortcake halves, cut side down. Spoon remaining strawberry mixture and whipped cream evenly over each serving. Yield: 9 servings.

Crazy Horse Campground

2113 Crazy Horse Road • Ashland, IL 62612
217-886-2089 • www.crazyhorsecamp.com

Located north of Jacksonville and west of Springfield, Crazy Horse Campground is a family oriented Illinois campground with lots of space to run and play. Whether you want to fish from their stocked ponds, participate in planned crafts and activities, play disc golf, listen to live music, swim with your kids, or relax by the fire, Crazy Horse offers fun for every member

of the family. Our camp store offers snacks, drinks, sundrys, and hot food, not to mention firewood and ice. Make your reservations in advance, particularly for holiday weekends, because everyone enjoys a visit to Crazy Horse Campground.

Apple Crisps

4 small apples, cored, peeled and thinly sliced
¼ cup instant oatmeal
¼ cup all-purpose flour
⅓ cup firmly packed light brown sugar
½ teaspoon ground cinnamon
¼ teaspoon ground nutmeg
1½ tablespoons melted butter

Preheat oven to 375°. Spray an 8x8-inch baking dish with nonstick cooking spray; spread apples evenly in bottom. In a bowl, thoroughly combine oatmeal, flour, sugar, cinnamon, nutmeg and butter. Sprinkle mixture over apples; bake 30 minutes or until apples are tender and topping is golden brown.

Forest View Farms

16717 South Lockwood Avenue • Tinley Park, IL 60477
708-560-0306 • www.fvfarms.com • Find us on Facebook

Forest View Farms, a locally owned, family-friendly horse and petting farm, has been bringing people and horses together since the 1950's. From the heated barn and indoor arena that allow year-round riding to the week-long summer camp that teaches you the true meaning of farm life, this is something you won't want to miss. The farm is contiguous to the Cook County Forest Preserve that provides boarders and trail riders with direct access to miles of beautiful trails for your horseback riding pleasure. Don't miss the Fall Festival, featuring the pumpkin patch so you may pick out your Halloween jack-o'-lantern, and a haunted hayride pursued by a headless horseman. The farm is also home to several white horses with historic legacies, one of which is a sixth-generation descendant of the horse, Silver, in the original *Lone Ranger* series. Another was used in the movie, *The Horse Whisperer*, starring Robert Redford.

Monday–Friday: 9:00 am to 7:00 pm
Saturday & Sunday: 8:00 am to 7:00 pm

Bread Pudding

8 large eggs
3½ cups whole milk
1½ cups whipping cream
1 teaspoon cinnamon
2 cups sugar
1 teaspoon vanilla extract
1 (1-pound) loaf French or Italian bread,, torn into cubes
1 cup golden raisins

Preheat oven to 350°. In a bowl, beat eggs well; add milk, cream, cinnamon, sugar and vanilla. Add bread and raisins; mix well. Pour into a buttered 9x13-inch pan. Bake until puffed and golden brown. Serve with Rum Sauce.

Rum Sauce:

1 cup brown sugar
½ cup butter
½ cup whipping cream
2 tablespoons dark rum
¾ teaspoon cinnamon

In a saucepan over medium heat, stir butter and sugar until smooth. Add cream, rum and cinnamon; simmer until reduced by half. Serve warm. Keeps 2 days, refrigerated. Warm before serving.

Knight's Action Park

Knight's Action Park

7 Days a Week

1700 Knights Recreation Drive • Springfield, IL 62711
217-546-8881 • www.knightsactionpark.com
www.route66-drivein.com • Find us on Facebook

Fun is the name of the game at Knight's Action Park. Knight's is open all year long because of the many things to do. Fun rules with a dry park, waterpark, and the Route 66 Drive-In Theater. The entire family loves the fifty-tee driving range (ten are heated for winter fun), batting cages, arcade games, and the two miniature golf courses. Enjoy the Kart track, the Paratrooper, and the Big Wheel. In the summer, enjoy all the wet action anyone could stand. Enjoy the Wave Pool, Action River, waterslides, thrill slides and kiddie pools or jump on a four-seat pedal boat. There's something for everyone at Knight's Action Park. Knight's welcomes guests of all ages to where the fun rules.

Doughnut Bread Pudding with Cinnamon Crème Anglaise

5 cups sugar
20 large eggs, beaten
1 tablespoon ground cinnamon
7 cups heavy cream
8 teaspoons pure vanilla extract

2 dozen doughnuts
4 cups packed light brown sugar
1 cup butter, softened
4 cups chopped pecans

Preheat oven to 350°. In a bowl, mix sugar, eggs, cinnamon and cream; add vanilla. Place doughnuts in a separate bowl. Pour egg mixture over doughnuts; let sit 10 minutes. In another bowl, mix and crumble together brown sugar, butter and pecans. Pour bread mixture into prepared pan; sprinkle brown sugar mixture over top. Bake 35 to 45 minutes or until set. Remove from oven.

Crème Anglaise:

2 whole vanilla beans, seeds and pods
3 cups heavy cream
3 cups milk

1½ cups sugar
½ teaspoon cinnamon
16 egg yolks

Split vanilla beans; scrape seeds into a medium saucepan and add pods to pan. Add cream, milk, sugar and cinnamon. Heat over medium-low heat until warm and sugar has dissolved. Whisk egg yolks in separate heatproof bowl. Slowly add half the warm cream to egg yolks, whisking constantly. Add egg and cream mixture back into saucepan; heat on medium low until cream becomes thick enough to coat back of a spoon or a thermometer inserted registers 180°. Strain through a sieve, removing vanilla bean pods to discard. Chill until ready to serve over individual platings of Doughnut Bread Pudding.

Chef De Cuisine Zac Leepper
Danenberger Family Vineyards

Chocolate Chip Pudding

¼ cup shortening
¼ cup sugar
¼ cup brown sugar
1 egg, beaten
¼ teaspoon salt
2½ teaspoons baking powder
⅓ cup whole milk
1½ cups flour
⅔ cup chocolate chips
¾ cup light corn syrup
¾ cup evaporated milk
2 tablespoons butter
1 teaspoon vanilla

In a mixing bowl with electric mixer, cream shortening and sugars; beat in egg. Continue to beat well while adding salt and baking powder. Blend in whole milk; mix in flour. Stir in chocolate chips; pour mixture into an 8x8-inch baking pan. Bake at 350° for 30 minutes. While cake is baking, in a saucepan over low heat, combine corn syrup, evaporated milk and butter, stirring constantly until butter is melted. Add vanilla at the end. Cut a square of cooled cake, place in bowl; pour a generous portion of the sauce over it. Scoop it up and spread on your thighs to get it where it's going more quickly.

Hornbaker Gardens

Candy Coal

Butter
2 cups sugar
½ cup water
¾ cup light brown sugar
1 teaspoon anise extract
½ teaspoon black paste food coloring

Line 8-inch square baking pan with foil, extending edges over sides of pan. Lightly grease foil with butter. In a heavy 2-quart saucepan over medium-low heat, cook sugar, corn syrup and water until sugar is dissolved and comes to a boil; cook 15 minutes without stirring until candy thermometer registers 290°.. Remove from heat immediately; stir in anise extract and food coloring. Pour mixture into prepared pan; cool completely. Lift candy out of pan using foil. Place candy between 2 layers of heavy-duty foil. Pound with mallet to break candy into 1 to 2 inch pieces.

City of West Frankfort

City of West Frankfort
and Chamber of Commerce

201 East Nolan • West Frankfort, IL 62896
Chamber of Commerce: 618-932-2181
www.westfrankfort-il.com • Find us on Facebook

When you visit West Frankfort, make your first stop the WF Outlet Mall, one of the country's top VF Factory Outlets. West Frankfort's rich coal mining history is evident when you visit Coal Miners Memorial Park downtown. The park features the Orient #2 Memorial, dedicated to the 119 coal miners who lost their lives in one of the largest mine disasters in United States history. Learn more about West Frankfort's coal mining history at the Frankfort Area Historical Museum, open each Wednesday, early March through mid-December. The museum features three floors of historical displays, including the Frankfort Area Genealogical Society. In mid-May, the Old King Coal Festival celebrates the city's coal mining history with four days of fun. The beautiful city park offers picnicking, fishing, and an indoor swimming pool and exercise center at the Aquatic and Recreation Center. Play a round of golf on the beautiful golf course at the Franklin County Country Club. Christmas Town comes alive at the Fantasy of Lights Parade on Tuesday before Thanksgiving and the opening of Candy Cane Lane in December.

Chamber
Tuesday, Wednesday & Thursday: 9:00 am to 4:00 pm

Sugar Crystals

You may know Sugar Crystals by their other name, Rock Candy, or perhaps by their most common adjective, delicious!

1 cup water	**Clean glass jar**
3 cups sugar	**Cotton string or yarn**
Pencil	**Food coloring, optional**

In a saucepan, boil water; stir in sugar 1 spoonful at a time, making sure it dissolves completely. While water is boiling, tie pencil to string long enough to hang down in jar without touching bottom or sides. Add a few drops of food coloring if you want your rocks to be colored. Carefully pour sugar solution into jar. Balance pencil with string tied to it on lip of jar, letting string dangle into solution. Store jar in a safe place; leave overnight. Sugar Crystals should begin to form on string by next day. Let sit until desired size is reached or crystals have finished growing. Remove from jar; let dry. Enjoy the sugary goodness.

Dave's "Down to Earth" Rock Shop

Dave's "Down to Earth" Rock Shop & Prehistoric Life Museum

711 Main Street • Evanston, IL 60202
847-866-7374 • www.davesrockshop.com • Find us on Facebook

Started in 1970, Dave and Sandy Douglass opened this unique shop specializing in selling art and treasures created by Mother Nature. Dave's offers their customers beautiful mineral and fossil specimens, jewelry created with semiprecious stones, and unique Native American artistry. Dave and Sandy began this adventure by fossil collecting in the Mazon Creek area of Illinois. After many years of self-collecting and other fossil-finding trips, they had amassed such a sizable collection that they opened a museum displaying the largest private collection of fossils representing every geological time period on display to the general public. Today the store is owned and operated by Sandy's brother, Jamie, and his wife, Susanne. You can truly take your children to a place back in time that teaches them about natural treasures of the past. Admission is free.

Monday, Tuesday & Friday: 10:30 am to 5:30 pm
Thursday: 10:30 am to 7:00 pm
Saturday: 10:00 am to 5:00 pm

Salty Caramel Sauce

Whimsical Candy serves this sauce as a snack during caramel-making class, spooned over house-made marshmallows or fresh green grapes and sprinkled with toasted pecans. It is also delicious on ice cream, of course.

3 tablespoons water
½ cup sugar
1½ tablespoons butter, softened
½ cup heavy cream, warmed
1 teaspoon vanilla extract (or ¼ fresh vanilla bean, scraped)
1 teaspoon sea salt

In a saucepan over medium heat, mix water and sugar; cook with minimal stirring until golden brown. (The color of sugar determines the flavor of your caramel. For a deeper flavor, cook to a slightly darker brown color.) Remove from heat. Whisk in butter. Stream in cream. Whisk to combine. Return to heat. Bring just to boil. Remove from heat again. Add vanilla and salt. Use warm, or cool for later use.

Whimsical Candy

Whimsical Candy

175 North Franklin Street, Lower Level • Chicago, IL 60606
312-781-0053 • www.whimsicalcandy.com

Whimsical Candy is a small-batch sweets company based on a lifelong love of candy. At age three, its founder packed her little pink suitcase and ran away to the candy store. Now a trained pastry chef, she and her team create handmade candies that blend the flavors and textures of nostalgic childhood candy with a grown-up taste for the highest-quality ingredients. Located in an historic candy factory, Whimsical Candy is the only working candy kitchen in Chicago's downtown Loop neighborhood. House-made specialties include La-Dee-Dahs (handmade swirls of nougat and caramel dipped in chocolate), ten unique candy bars, marshmallows, caramels, and fruit chews. Fresh seasonal goodies include ice cream sandwiches in the summer and caramel apples in autumn. See the candymakers in action, or schedule a candy-making class during your next trip to Chicago.

Monday–Friday: 11:00 am to 5:30 pm

Chocolate Lasagna

1 (14.3-ounce) package Oreo cookies, crushed in food processor
6 tablespoons butter, melted
1 (8-ounce) package cream cheese, softened
3¼ cups plus 2 tablespoons cold milk, divided
¼ cup sugar
1 (8-ounce) carton Cool Whip, divided
1 (3.9-ounce) package instant chocolate pudding
1½ cups mini chocolate chips

In a bowl, combine crushed cookies and butter. Press into bottom of a 9x13-inch baking dish and refrigerate. Using an electric mixer, beat cream cheese until light and fluffy; mix in 2 tablespoons milk and sugar. Fold in 1¼ cups Cool Whip. Spread over crust; put back in refrigerator. In a bowl, combine chocolate pudding with remaining milk; whisk until mixture starts to set. Spread over cream cheese mixture; refrigerate at least 5 minutes. Top with remaining Cool Whip; garnish with chocolate chips. Refrigerate until ready to serve.

Timber Ridge Outpost & Cabins

Timber Ridge Outpost & Cabins

Open All Year

North Iron Furnace Road • Karbers Ridge, IL 62955
GPS: 37°33'46.9" N
88°20'20.3" W
618-264-9091 • www.TimberRidgeOutpost.com

Timber Ridge Outpost & Cabins is Illinois' first and only tree house and log cabin resort, nestled in the Illinois Ozarks. This region of southern Illinois is best known for the famous Camel Rock at Garden of the Gods, just five minutes from Timber Ridge. Do something different this year! Stay in a luxurious tree house or log cabin near the Shawnee National Forest. It's an experience you won't soon forget! We offer two real treehouses, two modern log cabins, an authentic antique log cabin circa 1852 featuring a tree deck and two modern homes on acreage: Walnut Hill, a 2300 s.f. 4 bedroom/2 bath home on thirty-five private acres, and Pine Ridge Home, a 2-bedroom home on four private acres with a hot tub! Timber Ridge Outpost & Cabins offers a unique experience for families, honeymooners, hunters, fisherman, hikers, bird watchers, and stargazers. Nestled in the beautiful hills of the Shawnee National Forest, Timber Ridge Outpost & Cabins offers a unique experience for everyone with on-site activities and privately guided hikes and mushroom hunts. Or sign up for a round of archery golf, only at Timber Ridge Outpost & Cabins.

Chocolate Chip Cookies

¾ **cup granulated sugar**
¾ **cup brown sugar**
½ **cup shortening**
½ **cup butter**
½ **cup whole eggs**
½ **teaspoon pure vanilla extract**
½ **teaspoon salt**
¼ **teaspoon baking soda**
1½ **cups cake flour**
1½ **cups chocolate chips**

Preheat oven to 350°. Using a stand mixer, cream sugars, shortening and butter on low speed until smooth; scrape bowl. Add eggs, vanilla, salt and baking soda. Mix until liquid is incorporated; scrape bowl again. Add flour and chocolate chips; mix until dough forms. Drop dough onto parchment paper-lined cookie sheet with pastry bag or a medium scoop. Bake 12 minutes or until golden brown around edges. Yields roughly 32 cookies.

Roeser's Bakery

Roeser's Bakery

3216 West North Avenue • Chicago, IL 60647
773-489-6900 • www.roeserscakes.com

Since 1911, Roeser's Bakery has been producing the finest quality baked goods available. Started by John C. Roeser Sr., the bakery is now in its fourth generation with John C. Roeser IV guiding the way. Whether you're craving cake, cookies, donuts, ice cream, coffee cakes, bread, or just about any other assorted pastry, this full-line bakery is the place to find it—all made fresh from scratch daily. Come see for yourself why Roeser's Bakery has become a Chicago institution.

Tuesday–Saturday: 6:00 am to 8:00 pm
Sunday: 6:00 am to 6:00 pm
Monday: Closed

Large Chocolate Chip Cookies

1 pound margarine
2 cups brown sugar
1½ cups granulated sugar, plus more for cookie tops
3 eggs
2 tablespoons vanilla
6 cups all-purpose flour
1½ teaspoons baking soda
1½ teaspoons salt
2 (12-ounce) bags chocolate chips
2 (8-ounce) bags pecan pieces

Preheat oven to 350°. In a large bowl, cream margarine, sugars, eggs and vanilla. Sift together flour, baking soda and salt; add to creamed mixture. Fold in chips and pecans. Drop by large spoonful onto baking sheet. Bake 7 minutes. Do not overbake. Remove cookies to cooling racks and sprinkle tops with sugar.

ACM Tours

ACM Tours

Experience Illinois Amish Country

138 South Vine Street • Arthur, IL 61911
217-543-2766 • www.acmtours.com • Find us on Facebook

The Arthur Illinois Amish Settlement offers a culinary and cultural experience like no other. Hearty Amish cooking, a horse-and-buggy lifestyle, and a scenic rural landscape dotted with silos and country shops offer an experience you will remember. Browse the shops in Arthur and the surrounding Amish countryside to learn about the Amish people and their lifestyle. Take a self-guided audio tour or a ride-along guide to find out how and why the Amish choose to live without electricity or automobiles. For a more personal experience, ACM Tours can schedule a family-style meal with an Amish family in their home and a tour of their farm. For a full overview of Illinois Amish Country and our full calendar of events visit www.IllinoisAmishCountry.com.

Monday–Saturday: 9:00 am to 5:00 pm

Frozen Toasted Almond Balls with Hot Fudge

1 quart French vanilla ice cream
2 cups chopped toasted almonds
1 cup cocoa
2 cups brown sugar
1 cup white sugar
⅛ teaspoon salt
2 tablespoons cornstarch
2 cups water
3 tablespoons butter
1 teaspoon vanilla

Shape ice cream into balls; roll in almonds. Place balls in freezer until ready to serve. Sift together cocoa, sugars, salt, cornstarch and water; place in saucepan over medium heat. Stir to mix. Bring to a boil; reduce heat to low. Cook until mixture thickens to consistency of thick cream. Remove from heat; add butter and vanilla, stirring well. Remove ice cream balls from freezer; place in serving dish. Drizzle hot fudge over top. Serve immediately.

Wabash Depot Antique Centre

780 East Cerro Gordo Street • Decatur, IL 62523
217-233-0800 • Find us on Facebook

Wabash Depot Antique Centre is located in the old Wabash Train Depot, listed on the National Register of Historic Places. In 1901, architect Theodore Link designed the two-story building in the classical Revival Style, made of yellow brick and limestone with terra cotta and sandstone trim. First-floor windows have arched sandstone frames and sills, and two terra cotta belt courses circle the building above and below the second floor. It closed as a passenger station in 1985 but was restored and reopened as the Wabash Depot Antique Centre in 2002. You can wander from room to room and enjoy the building or shop for hours in the 10,000 square feet of antiques and treasures. Experience antique shopping like never before. Friendly, helpful staff are always willing to assist you with your purchases in and out of the building. Wabash Depot Antique Centre's Anniversary Open House is the first weekend in June and Holiday Open House is the first weekend in November.

Monday–Saturday: 10:00 am to 5:00 pm
Sunday: Noon to 5:00 pm

Caramelized Bananas

3 large firm bananas
3 tablespoons butter
3 tablespoons packed light brown sugar
1 tablespoon rum or brandy
½ cup vanilla yogurt
½ teaspoon nutmeg

Peel bananas and cut on a sharp diagonal into slices ½-inch thick. In a large heavy skillet over medium heat, cook butter and brown sugar, stirring constantly until sugar dissolves. Add bananas; cook uncovered, carefully turning once, until bananas are richly browned and caramelized on both sides. Push bananas to one side of pan, add rum, stirring to blend. Spoon bananas onto dessert plates, drizzling with sauce. Top with a spoonful of yogurt; dust with nutmeg. Serve.

Kishauwau Country Cabins

901 North 2129th Road • Tonica, IL 61370
815-442-8453 • www.kishauwaucabins.com

Kishauwau Country Cabins is Starved Rock area's best cabin rental destination. Explore the sixty-five beautiful wooded acres located on a bluff above the Vermillion River. The seventeen various sized cabins—3 are dog friendly—are able to accommodate any number, from large family reunions to a couple looking for a nice quiet getaway. The beautiful, rustically constructed cabins offer a blend of country charm with modern conveniences. The only items you'll need to bring are food, beverages, clothes, and of course the family and Fido. During the year there are many festivals and fairs, flea markets, auctions, and other local activities. Check out their schedule at our website: click on Things To Do and then Events for a list. So pack up the car and visit today.

Caramel Apples

10 Granny Smith apples, washed, well dried
2 (11-ounce) packages Kraft premium caramel bits
10 popsicle sticks
1 cup peanuts, chopped (optional)

Remove stems from apples; set aside. In a microwave-safe bowl, heat caramel bits in 30 second intervals until they reach workable consistency. Place popsicle stick in top of each apple. Dip one at a time, completely coating with caramel. Shake off excess caramel and roll in chopped peanuts, if desired. Place on parchment paper. Let cool and enjoy!

Windy City Sweets

Windy City Sweets

3308 North Broadway • Chicago, IL 60657
773-477-6100 • www.windycitysweets.com

Windy City Sweets was established in 1983 with a vision to create a Willy Wonka-esque experience for chocolate enthusiast and it's been a popular Chicago north side neighborhood destination ever since. With more than 1,200 different products, Windy City Sweets is proud to offer something to satisfy everyone's sweet tooth. One-of-a-kind chocolate creations are made on-site by innovative chocolatiers using Windy City Sweets' signature chocolate blend. Their popular handmade fudge is made in-house using only real ingredients. Windy City Sweets searches the globe for the highest quality nut varieties for your snacking pleasure, and offers a large selection of world-famous ice cream, sorbet, and yogurt. Windy City Sweets also offers gift boxes, gift tins, and gift baskets for purchase. Their Candy Concierges can help you create the perfect gift for holidays and special occasions or find just the right treat to make any day a celebration. You can call or stop by the store and leave the rest up to a Candy Concierge. Windy City Sweets makes life sweeter every day.

Daily: 11:00 am to 10:00 pm

Strawberry Sorbet Bellini

½ cup water
1 cup sugar
1 pound fresh strawberries, washed and hulled
¼ cup lemon juice
Pinch salt
⅓ cup Prosecco Italian sparkling wine

In a medium saucepan over medium heat, bring water and sugar to a boil; simmer, stirring frequently, until sugar is completely dissolved. Remove from heat; allow to cool almost completely. In a food processor, pulse strawberries until broken down but still chunky. Add cooled syrup and remaining ingredients to processor with strawberries; continue to process until very smooth. Pour sorbet mixture into a 9-inch metal cake pan or other shallow, freezer-safe container; place in freezer. Every 30 minutes, remove sorbet from freezer; use a fork to break up, stir and smash chunks of sorbet. Smooth sorbet before returning to freezer. Repeat stirring process until mixture is completely frozen. To serve, scoop into cups or bowls and enjoy! Add fresh, thin-sliced strawberries for garnish.

Note: Prosecco will help to keep mixture from freezing solid. If you prefer to omit wine, it may be necessary to remove frozen sorbet from freezer about 15 minutes or so before serving. Peaches or mangoes can be substituted for strawberries, if desired.

Caffé Gelato

Caffé Gelato

2034 West Division Street • Chicago, IL 60622
773-227-7333 • www.caffegelatochicago.com • Find us on Facebook

Caffé Gelato provides the best gelato, sorbets, and coffee beverages in the beautiful city of Chicago. The coffee beans are roasted in the café every morning, giving Division Street an unbelievable aroma of fresh roasted coffee. The gelato and sorbets are made fresh daily using only the freshest fruits, nuts, and imported goods from Italy. Their high expectations are the foundation on which they prepare and serve gelato and coffees every day. The staff is trained to use the best ingredients and work on the finest machinery in order to produce the best product possible for their customers. Time and time again, customers have shared stories about how Caffé Gelato reminds them of their time studying abroad or vacationing and eating creamy gelato as they walked the streets of Florence, Rome, or Venice, and many other cities across Europe. Every day the goal remains the same: give all customers the best and most authentic gelato experience that would rival those in Europe.

Daily: 9:00 am to 9:00 pm

White Chocolate Popcorn with M&Ms

This is a delicious treat that is both salty and sweet.

Popcorn
Salt
1 (24-ounce) package white almond bark
1 (16-ounce) package plain M&Ms

Pop a large batch of popcorn and salt to taste; cool. Spread popcorn over wax paper on a flat surface or cookie sheet. Melt bark in microwave by cooking 2 minutes. Stir with a whisk. If lumpy, return to microwave in 20 second increments until completely smooth. While bark is melting, sprinkle M&Ms over popcorn. Pour white chocolate over popcorn, reserving about a quarter of the chocolate to drizzle at the end. Mix popcorn gently, rolling it around on pan to cover with bark. Using a spatula, drizzle reserved chocolate over popcorn and M&Ms. Cool and enjoy. Get creative! Add Andes Mint Candies for a minty treat or any other candy you can think of (the photo shows M&Ms and Andes Mint Candies).

FlutterBy Gourmet Popcorn LLC

FlutterBy Gourmet Popcorn LLC

621 Liberty Street • Morris, IL 60450
723 South Clark Street • North Utica, IL 61373
815-710-5070 • www.flutterbypopcorn.com • Find us on Facebook

FlutterBy Gourmet Popcorn LLC has been creating some of the freshest and tastiest popcorn since 2005. Drop in to enjoy free samples each day. Try Cheddar Cheese or Buttery Caramel. For the more adventurous, FlutterBy offers some of the most creative flavors around—Cookies & Cream, Reese's Peanut Butter Cups, Banana Cream Pie, Birthday Cake, Bacon Cheese, Spicy 5-Alarm, Garlic Parm, and so much more—50 flavors in all! You may also enjoy Cinnamon-coated Almonds, Cashews, and Pecans as well as Amish Cashew Crunch, fudge, and Amish popping products. FlutterBy prides itself on offering customers only the best gourmet popcorn made in small batches using only quality ingredients. Stop in, sample what they create, and take some home to share. You're in for a TREAT.

Order online at www.flutterbypopcorn.com!

Banana Split Pie

2 deep-dish pie shells
1 stick butter, softened
1 tablespoon vanilla
1 (16-ounce) package powdered sugar
1 (16-ounce) plus 1 (8-ounce) containers Cool Whip
1 (20-ounce) can crushed pineapple, well drained
4 large bananas, sliced
Crushed pecans, garnish
3 maraschino cherries, garnish

Bake pie shells per package directions; cool completely. In a large bowl, combine butter, vanilla, powdered sugar, containers of Cool Whip and pineapple; mix well. Fold in bananas. Pour into pie shells. Garnish with pecans. Top centers with cherries. Refrigerate until ready to serve.

Jimi Williams-Cox
Williams Hill Pass

Williams Hill Pass

Off-Highway Recreational Trails Park & Campground
Gateway to the Shawnee National Forest
1935 Peak Road • Harrisburg, IL 62946
618-252-6978 • www.williamshillpass.com • Find us on Facebook

Load up your friends, family, pets, ATVs, dirt bikes, side-by-sides, and camping gear for an outdoor vacation full of fun. Williams Hill Pass offers off-highway vehicle (OHV) riding opportunities for all ages and riding abilities, surrounded by a beautiful atmosphere and the Shawnee National Forest. Williams Hill Pass has a controlled atmosphere, which makes it a safe place for young children and families to ride. After a full day of riding, plan to stay. No reason to go home when you can relax and kick back in one of their cabins or at an electric or primitive campsite. Enjoy a blazing fire and outdoor cooking while absorbing the beauty of the outdoors. Gather your friends and family for a fun and relaxing stay at Williams Hill Pass.

Apple Pie

Crust:

1½ cups flour
1 tablespoon sugar
½ teaspoon salt
1 stick butter, cubed
2 tablespoons vegetable shortening
7 tablespoons ice water

In a large bowl, sift flour, sugar and salt. Using a pastry blender, incorporate butter and shortening until mixture looks like coarse meal. Add water, 1 tablespoon at a time. Shape into a round disk; wrap in plastic wrap. Refrigerate at least 20 minutes or until ready to use. Roll out half of dough into circle; lay over pie plate. Trim excess around rim and flute edges. Roll out remaining dough; cut in strips to make lattice. Set oven to 350° to preheat while preparing filling.

Filling:

1 Red Delicious apple
1 Golden Delicious apple
2 Granny Smith apples
4 Gala apples
½ cup butter
3 tablespoons flour
½ cup white sugar
½ cup packed brown sugar
½ tablespoon cinnamon
¼ cup water
Egg wash (1 egg beaten with 1 tablespoon water)

Cube apples in small cubes; mix together. Place apples in crust; make a lattice on top. In a saucepan over medium heat, melt butter; stir in flour. Add sugars, cinnamon and water; bring to a boil. Reduce to low; simmer 2 minutes. Add a little more water if sauce looks clumpy. Pour sugar mixture in middle of lattice, letting spread on its own. Brush any part of exposed pie crust with egg wash. Bake 50 minutes, checking often making sure top doesn't burn.

Andrea DiGangi
Five-time Apple Pie Baking Festival Champion
The Johnny Appleseed Festival

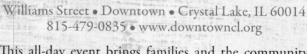

The Johnny Appleseed Festival

Last Saturday in September

Williams Street • Downtown • Crystal Lake, IL 60014
815-479-0835 • www.downtowncl.org

This all-day event brings families and the community together to celebrate Fall. The Johnny Appleseed Festival is jam-packed (apple jam, of course!) with great activities such as pony rides, petting zoo, wagon rides, pumpkin train, children's games, moonwalk, craft fair, pie baking contest, pumpkin bowling, storytelling, clowns, face painting, dancing, live music, great food, and even Johnny Appleseed himself! At 3:00 pm, join the excitement of the Great Ball Race on Brink Street, just east of Williams Street. Tickets will be available for sale at the Johnny Appleseed Festival. Grand prize is $1000. We guarantee—you won't want to miss the fun!

Libby's Famous Pumpkin Pie

¾ cup sugar
1 teaspoon ground cinnamon
½ teaspoon salt
½ teaspoon ground ginger
¼ teaspoon ground cloves
2 large eggs
1 (15-ounce) can Libby's 100% pure pumpkin
1 (12-ounce) can Nestlé's Carnation evaporated milk
1 (9-inch) deep-dish pie shell, unbaked
Whipped cream, optional

Preheat oven to 425°. Mix sugar, cinnamon, salt, ginger and cloves in a small bowl; set aside. In another bowl, beat eggs. Stir in pumpkin and sugar-spice mixture. Gradually stir in evaporated milk. Pour into pie shell. Bake 15 minutes; reduce temperature to 350° and bake 40 to 50 minutes or until knife inserted in center comes out clean. Cool on wire rack 2 hours. Serve immediately or refrigerate. Top with whipped cream before serving, if desired.

Morton Pumpkin Festival

Morton Pumpkin Festival

Mid-September

Downtown • Morton, IL 61550
309-263-2491 • www.mortonpumpkinfestival.org

In 1967, the first Morton Pumpkin Festival was organized by the Morton Chamber of Commerce. It has since become an annual celebration of the beginning of the pumpkin harvest and canning season at the village's local Libby's pumpkin plant. In 1978, the governor of Illinois signed a proclamation declaring Morton, Illinois, the "Pumpkin Capital of the World" since 85% of the world's canned pumpkin is processed in Morton. Today, the Morton Pumpkin Festival includes countless special events and venues organized and hosted by the Morton Chamber of Commerce and more than 2,000 volunteers. The Pumpkin Festival is held annually in mid-September and welcomes an estimated 70,000 visitors each year to enjoy pumpkin foods, live entertainment, parades, a 10K race, a carnival, and much more.

MORTON
CHAMBER of COMMERCE

Lemon Ice Box Pie

1 graham cracker pie crust
1 (8-ounce) package cream cheese, softened
1 (14-ounce) can sweetened condensed milk
3 egg yolks
Smidgen salt
1 teaspoon vanilla
⅔ cup fresh lemon juice

Preheat oven to 350°. Bake crust 5 minutes; remove and cool completely. In a bowl using an electric mixer, beat cream cheese until smooth. Add condensed milk, yolks, salt and vanilla; mix until velvety smooth. Add lemon juice; beat 1 minute. Immediately pour into cooled pie shell. Refrigerate until ready to serve.

Barnacopia

2570 North West Branch Road • Polo, IL 61064
815-238-1474 • www.Barnacopia.com

Barnacopia is a three-story museum featuring an incredible and unique collection of farm machinery, antique cars, and local nostalgia. It is housed in an old-style mortise-and-tenon timber-frame barn. One of the many highlights is the John Deere 730 tractor that rotates in the cupola. There is a passenger elevator servicing all three floors of the barn. The second floor has a "drive-in" movie theater with many classic cars in which to sit and watch the "movie." You can play pool on the John Deere pool table in the game room on the third floor. The attached silo serves as a bed-and-breakfast. Tours include a scoop of ice cream served in the ice-cream parlor. Barnacopia is also a great venue for business events, family gatherings, and weddings.

Pie Crust

2 cups flour
½ teaspoon salt
¾ cup shortening
2 tablespoons cup ice water
2 tablespoons cream

Preheat oven to 450°. In a bowl using your fingertips, rub flour, salt and shortening together to form a soft and rather damp mixture. Add water and mix to form a dough. Separate into 2 parts; chill 20 minutes. Remove crust from refrigerator and place on well-floured board. Dust rolling pin with flour. Roll each part as thin as possible. Lay crust in pie pans. Brush with cream to make a flaky, browned crust. Bake 12 to 18 minutes or until browned.

Lovin Oven Cakery

2207 North Route 83 • Round Lake Beach, IL 60073
847-231-4700 • www.lovinovencakery.com • Find us on Facebook

If baking is a lost art, Lovin Oven Cakery is the place to rediscover Old World pleasures. Four-time consecutive winner of Weddingwire Couple's Choice Award (2014–2017), Lovin Oven's delicious desserts are made from only the finest ingredients—thick and heavy cream, European-style butter, farm-fresh eggs, premium frostings, and the sweetest fruit fillings. Their dedication to providing the best baked goods available ensures you enjoy a fresh and pleasurable experience every time you visit. What sets them aside from the ordinary bakery? Attention to producing only the highest-quality product; allowing their talented staff artistic freedom; providing friendly, efficient, and helpful customer service; and offering a warm atmosphere to complete the experience. Come taste the difference pride makes.

Saturday: 6:00 am to 6:00 pm
Sunday: 8:00 am to 1:00 pm
Tuesday–Friday: 6:00 am to 7:00 pm

Index of Events & Destinations

C

D

Index of Recipes

Great American Cookbooks

Game for all Seasons Cookbook

$16.95 • 240 pages • 7x10
paperbound • full color

The Ultimate Venison Cookbook for Deer Camp

$21.95 • 288 pages • 7x10
paperbound • full color

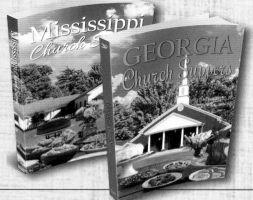

Church Recipes are the Best

Georgia Church Suppers
$18.95 • 256 pages • 7x10 • paperbound • full color

Mississippi Church Suppers
$21.95 • 288 pages • 7x10 • paperbound • full color

It's So Easy...

to Cook Food Your Family Will Love...

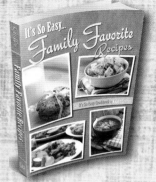

Family Favorite Recipes • Kitchen Memories
EACH: $18.95 • 256 pages • 7x10
paperbound • full color

Great American Grilling
$21.95 • 288 pages • 7x10
paperbound • full color

Great American Cookbooks

Little Gulf Coast Seafood Cookbook

$14.95 • 192 pages • 5½x8½
paperbound • full color

State Hometown Cookbook Series

A Hometown Taste of America, One State at a Time

Each state's charm is revealed through local recipes from resident cooks along with stories and photos that will take you back to your hometown ...or take you on a journey to explore other hometowns across the country.

EACH: $18.95 • 256 pages • 8x9 • paperbound • full color

Alabama • Georgia • Louisiana • Mississippi

South Carolina • Tennessee • Texas • West Virginia

State Back Road Restaurants Series

Every Road Leads to Delicious Food

From two-lane highways and interstates, to dirt roads and quaint downtowns, every road leads to delicious food when traveling across our United States. Each well-researched and charming guide leads you to the state's best back road restaurants. No time to travel? No problem. Each restaurant shares their favorite recipes—their signature dish, or a family favorite, always delicious.

EACH: $18.95 • 256 pages • 7x9 • paperbound • full color

Alabama • Kentucky • Missouri • Tennessee • Texas

www.GreatAmericanPublishers.com • www.facebook.com/GreatAmericanPublishers

Eat & Explore Cookbook Series

Explore the distinct flavor of each state by savoring 200 favorite local recipes. In addition, fun festivals, exciting events, unique attractions, and fascinating tourist destinations are profiled throughout the book with everything you need to plan your family's next getaway.

This series is a favorite of local cooks, armchair travelers, and cookbook collectors across the nation.
EACH: $18.95 • 256 pages • 7x9 • paperbound

**Arkansas • Illinois • Minnesota • North Carolina
Ohio • Oklahoma • Virginia • Washington**

ORDER FORM

Mail to: Great American Publishers • 501 Avalon Way Suite B • Brandon, MS 39047
Or call us toll-free 1.888.854.5954 to order by check or credit card

❏ Check Enclosed

Charge to: ❏ Visa ❏ MC ❏ AmEx ❏ Disc

Card #

Exp Date / Signature

Name

Address

City/State _____ Zip

Phone

Email

Qty.	Title	Total
	Subtotal	

Postage ($4.00 first book; $1.00 each additional;
Order 4 or more books, FREE SHIPPING)

Total